CREATIONISM
VS. EVOLUTION

CREATIONISM VS. EVOLUTION

Other Books in the At Issue Series:

CREATIONISM VS. EVOLUTION

Bruno J. Leone, *Book Editor*

Daniel Leone, *Publisher*
Bonnie Szumski, *Editorial Director*
Scott Barbour, *Managing Editor*

An Opposing Viewpoints® Series

Greenhaven Press, Inc.
San Diego, California

Library of Congress Cataloging-in-Publication Data

Creationism vs. evolution / Bruno J. Leone, book editor.
    p. cm. — (At issue series)
    Includes bibliographical references and index.
    ISBN 0-7377-0795-X (alk. paper) —
ISBN 0-7377-0794-1 (pbk. : alk. paper)
    1. Creationism. 2. Evolution—Religious aspects. I. Title:
Creationism versus evolution. II. Leone, Bruno J., 1939– III. At
issue (San Diego, Calif.)

BS652 .C74   2002
231.7'652—dc21   2001023881
                                                                      CIP

Table of Contents

Introduction

"Creationism is the doctrine that matter and all things were created, substantially as they now exist, by an omnipotent Creator, and not gradually evolved or developed."

"Evolution is the continuous genetic adaptation of organisms or species to the environment by the integrating agencies of selection, hybridization, inbreeding, and mutation."

Webster's Encyclopedic Unabridged Dictionary of the English Language, First Edition, 1989

In August 1925, John T. Scopes, a teacher from Dayton, Tennessee, was brought to trial for teaching Charles Darwin's theory of evolution to his high school biology students. The teaching of evolution violated a Tennessee state law which mandated that in Tennessee public schools only divine creation could be presented by teachers as an explanation for the origin and development of life on earth.

The John T. Scopes trial

When Scopes announced that the gifted and nationally famous criminal defense lawyer Clarence Darrow would be defending him, the prosecution secured the services of an equally prominent attorney, William Jennings Bryan. The prospect of two of America's greatest legal minds facing off in court on so controversial an issue instantly turned the trial into a national media event. Journalists from throughout the United States and several foreign countries descended upon the little town of Dayton to witness this battle between Darrow and Bryan. Although Scopes was ultimately found guilty, throughout the trial a much larger issue overshadowed the defendant's innocence or guilt, the question of Christian fundamentalism versus scientific modernism. Bryan, as the champion of fundamentalism, showed up in court each day with a King James bible in hand. For every argument by Clarence Darrow supporting the theory of evolution or, at very least, the right to teach evolution and similar scientific theories, Bryan would find an appropriate passage in his bible to refute the defense attorney's claims. For his part, Darrow countered prosecution arguments with what he contended was credible scientific evidence directly challenging Bryan's biblical literalism.

The courtroom battle between Darrow and Bryan was bitter and savage. It proved a watershed in what has been an ongoing battle between proponents and opponents of the concept of evolution. And although more than seventy-five years have passed since the Scopes trial, the issues debated in that Tennessee courtroom resonate today as the controversy continues to rage.

The struggle between supporters and critics of evolutionary theory appears irreconcilable. Science has found in Darwinian evolution a grand unifying principle that credibly explains how life in all its varied forms changed and adapted to its environment. Conversely, Christian fundamentalism has identified in Darwinian evolution a profane principle, which denies God a role in the creation and progression of life.

Genesis and creation

The controversy arises from the fundamentalist interpretation of the Bible, specifically Genesis, the first book of Scriptures. In Genesis, God is depicted as creating the heavens and the earth and all living things inhabiting the earth in a six-day time frame. Christian fundamentalists interpret this literally as six, twenty-four hour segments of time (one week less one day). What fundamentalists also extract from Genesis is that God was satisfied with his creation and created nothing new after those first six days. Therefore, accepting the Bible's assumption that history began on the sixth day with the creation of Adam and Eve, the first man and woman, the only conclusion available is that the earth and all it contains are relatively young and unchanging. In fact in 1650, James Usher, an Irish archbishop and scholar, used information gleaned from the Bible to calculate that God created the earth in 4004 B.C.

Science on the other hand places the age of the earth at 4½ to 5 billion years, with simple, unicellular life first appearing approximately 2½ billion years ago. According to Darwinian theory, it was from these first unicellular life forms that ultimately *all* living things evolved, including humans.

The concept underlying Darwin's evolutionary mechanism is quite simple: Over time, gradual changes continually occur in the physical makeup of plants and animals. Genetic mutations and other factors are responsible for these changes. If the changes are great enough and happen over a long enough period of time, a new species will eventually evolve provided that the plant or animal survives the changes. Finally, while the Bible attributes all of creation to God's intelligent design, science sees blind chance as the only driving force behind evolutionary change.

Fundamentalist reaction to Darwin

The initial reaction of Christian fundamentalists to Darwin's theory of evolution was understandable and predictable. (Darwin's book, *The Origin of Species*, was first published in 1859.) Since evolution totally contradicted the bedrock of Christianity, namely the belief in a creator God who chose to remain involved in His creation, it should not be taught in science classes to impressionable school children. Christian fundamentalists in the United States, therefore, responded to the teaching of evolution in public schools by lobbying state legislatures to create laws that would exclude evolution from school curricula. The Tennessee state law resulting in John Scopes's trial and conviction for teaching evolution was a product of those lobbying efforts.

In response to the fundamentalist initiative, state and national organizations of scientists and teachers of science started lobbying themselves, their efforts intensifying in the late 1940s and 1950s. As these scientists began meeting with success and evolution became a universal part of science curricula in schools throughout the country, fundamentalists were compelled to rethink their tactics. The result was the formal and informal organization of groups of Christian scientists throughout the country, each dedicated to supporting and perpetuating the belief in divine creation. Referred to as scientific creationists, their strategy was to demand equal time in the classroom for their fundamentalist views. Their rationale was unpretentious and disarming. Claiming that since both evolution and divine creation cannot be proven in the laboratory, neither should take precedence over the other in the classroom. Rather, both should be part of the science curriculum.

Creation science uses science

However, the real thrust of creation science was (and remains) to rely upon science itself to compromise and disprove evolution. Scientific creationists, many of whom hold advanced degrees in various sciences from major universities throughout the United States and the world, no longer enter classrooms or other public forums armed only with their bibles. Capitalizing upon the results of their own scientific research, creationists argue that they have breached all of the evolutionists' principle arguments.

For example, traditional science has relied upon various chronometrical (time measurement) techniques to date prehistoric fossils. One popular method is carbon 14 (C14). C14 is a radioactive isotope, which enters the earth's atmosphere in steady amounts and is absorbed and measurable in all living things. However, when a plant or animal dies, C14 is no longer absorbed. Instead, the remains of the plant or animal loses half of its C14 every 5,730 years. After about 50,000 years, the amounts of C14 remaining in a fossilized specimen are too small to measure. Archaeologists have used the C14 dating method to accurately date fossils up to nearly 50,000 years old. Because of its accuracy, C14 is paraded before the public as undeniable proof of the existence of prehistoric life. Creation science has countered that the validity of C14 depends upon measuring the intensity of cosmic radiation presently in the atmosphere. If that intensity was different in the distant past, then the C14 methodology will be incorrect in its measurements. Since it is impossible to measure the intensity of cosmic radiation in the past, scientific creationists contend that C14 dating is an invalid technique.

Scientific creationists also have homed in on what they claim is the mathematical impossibility of complicated organs such as the eye evolving in gradual increments. Since a myriad of variable and complex factors account for a functioning eye, it is impossible, they say, for the eye to have evolved by pure chance. Scientists, however, refute this claim by arguing that given the enormous amount of time available (the evolutionary time scale encompasses hundreds of millions of years), the possibility of organs such as the eye forming by the process of gradual evolution is high. In fact, scientists maintain that computer models, which condense millions of years of geologic time into a relatively short computer program, have demonstrated this likelihood.

There are numerous other areas where scientific creationists have relied upon their own research to refute the claims of evolutionists. But mainstream science always seems poised and eager to respond to each challenge.

Theistic evolution

Fairly recently, however, another school of thought has entered the fray. Referred to as theistic evolution, this alternative combines elements essential to both evolutionary theory and creation science. Theistic evolution accepts the basic axiom of evolution while contending that God is the directing force behind it. Although the concept of theistic evolution is as old as the evolution/creationism controversy, in the last ten years it has grown in credibility and attracted many more adherents among scientists, theologians, and laypersons. In fact in October 1996, Pope John Paul II, speaking for the world's nearly 1 billion Roman Catholics, sent a message to the Pontifical Academy of Sciences in which he wrote: "New knowledge has led to the recognition of more than one hypothesis in the theory of evolution. It is indeed remarkable that this theory has been progressively accepted by researchers following a series of discoveries in various fields of knowledge. The convergence, neither sought nor fabricated, of the results of work that was conducted independently is in itself a significant argument in favor of this theory." The pope went on to say that as long as God is recognized as the instigator and guiding force behind evolution, then evolution can be accepted as consistent with Christian belief. Religious leaders representing other large segments of the Judeo-Christian world have been echoing John Paul's sentiments for many years.

Ironically, on the issue of creationism versus evolution, most Americans appear to fall into one of the three categories outlined above. An article appearing in a recent issue of the *Los Angeles Times* cites polls showing that scientific creationism and theistic evolution have equal numbers of adherents among the American public (approximately 45 percent each). The remaining 10 percent believe that all life is the product of evolutionary chance, not cosmic design. *At Issue: Creationism vs. Evolution* presents arguments by proponents representing all sides in this ongoing controversy.

1

Gradual Change Explains How Evolution Works

Richard Dawkins

Richard Dawkins is the author of the widely acclaimed book, The Blind Watchmaker. *A resident of Oxford, England, he holds the first Charles Simonyi chair of Public Understanding of Science at Oxford University.*

Opponents of evolution typically cite the eye in an effort to discredit the concept of evolution; the intricacy of the eye and its complex relationship to other parts of the anatomy can only be explained by intelligent design, opponents argue, not evolutionary happenstance. However, given the enormity of the geological time scale, time favors the gradual evolution of any anatomical part, including the eye. Studies have been conducted in which computer models have simulated the evolution of the eye in gradual increments. The success of these studies underscores the premise that chance and gradualism can and do account for evolutionary change.

Mention of poor eyes and good eyes brings me to the creationist's favorite conundrum. What is the use of half an eye? How can natural selection favor an eye that is less than perfect? I have treated the question before and have laid out a spectrum of intermediate eyes, drawn from those that actually exist in the various phyla of the animal kingdom. Here I shall incorporate eyes in the rubric I have established of theoretical gradients. There is a gradient, a continuum, of tasks for which an eye might be used. I am at present using my eyes for recognizing letters of the alphabet as they appear on a computer screen. You need good, high-acuity eyes to do that. I have reached an age when I can no longer read without the aid of glasses, at present quite weakly magnifying ones. As I get older still, the strength of my prescription will steadily mount. Without my glasses, I shall find it gradually and steadily harder to see close detail. Here we have yet another continuum—a continuum of age.

Vision varies between species

Any normal human, however old, has better vision than an insect. There are tasks that can be usefully accomplished by people with relatively poor vision, all the way down to the nearly blind. You can play tennis with quite blurry vision, because a tennis ball is a large object, whose position and movement can be seen even if it is out of focus. Dragonflies' eyes, though poor by our standards, are good by insect standards, and dragonflies can hawk for insects on the wing, a task about as difficult as hitting a tennis ball. Much poorer eyes could be used for the task of avoiding crashing into a wall or walking over the edge of a cliff or into a river. Eyes that are even poorer could tell when a shadow, which might be a cloud but could also portend a predator, looms overhead. And eyes that are still poorer could serve to tell the difference between night and day, which is useful for, among other things, synchronizing breeding seasons and knowing when to go to sleep. There is a continuum of tasks to which an eye might be put, such that for any given quality of eye, from magnificent to terrible, there is a level of task at which a marginal improvement in vision would make all the difference. There is therefore no difficulty in understanding the gradual evolution of the eye, from primitive and crude beginnings, through a smooth continuum of intermediates, to the perfection we see in a hawk or in a young human.

There is therefore no difficulty in understanding the gradual evolution of the eye, from primitive and crude beginnings, through a smooth continuum of intermediates, to the perfection we see in a hawk or in a young human.

Thus the creationist's question—"What is the use of half an eye?"—is a lightweight question, a doddle to answer. Half an eye is just 1 percent better than 49 percent of an eye, which is already better than 48 percent, and the difference is significant. A more ponderous show of weight seems to lie behind the inevitable supplementary: "Speaking as a physicist,* I cannot believe that there has been enough time for an organ as complicated as the eye to have evolved from nothing. Do you really think there has been enough time?" Both questions stem from the Argument from Personal Incredulity. Audiences nevertheless appreciate an answer, and I have usually fallen back on the sheer magnitude of geological time. If one pace represents one century, the whole of Anno Domini time is telescoped into a cricket pitch. To reach the origin of multicellular animals on the same scale, you'd have to slog all the way from New York to San Francisco.

*I hope this does not give offense. In support of my point, I cite the following from *Science and Christian Belief*, by a distinguished physicist, the Reverend John Polkinghorne (1994, p. 16): "Someone like Richard Dawkins can present persuasive pictures of how the sifting and accumulation of small differences can produce large-scale developments, but, instinctively, a physical scientist would like to see an estimate, however rough, of how many steps would take us from a slightly light-sensitive cell to a fully formed insect eye, and of approximately the number of generations required for the necessary mutations to occur."

It now appears that the shattering enormity of geological time is a steamhammer to crack a peanut. Trudging from coast to coast dramatizes the time *available* for the evolution of the eye. But a recent study by a pair of Swedish scientists, Dan Nilsson and Susanne Pelger, suggests that a ludicrously small fraction of that time would have been plenty. When one says "the" eye, by the way, one implicitly means the vertebrate eye, but serviceable image-forming eyes have evolved between forty and sixty times, independently from scratch, in many different invertebrate groups. Among these forty-plus independent evolutions, at least nine distinct design principles have been discovered, including pinhole eyes, two kinds of camera-lens eyes, curved-reflector ("satellite dish") eyes, and several kinds of compound eyes. Nilsson and Pelger have concentrated on camera eyes with lenses, such as are well developed in vertebrates and octopuses.

A telling study

How do you set about estimating the time required for a given amount of evolutionary change? We have to find a unit to measure the size of each evolutionary step, and it is sensible to express it as a percentage change in what is already there. Nilsson and Pelger used the number of successive changes of 1 percent as their unit for measuring changes of anatomical quantities. This is just a convenient unit—like the calorie, which is defined as the amount of energy needed to do a certain amount of work. It is easiest to use the 1 percent unit when the change is all in one dimension. In the unlikely event, for instance, that natural selection favored bird-of-paradise tails of ever-increasing length, how many steps would it take for the tail to evolve from one meter to one kilometer in length? A 1 percent increase in tail length would not be noticed by the casual bird-watcher. Nevertheless, it takes surprisingly few such steps to elongate the tail to one kilometer—fewer than seven hundred.

It takes surprisingly few such steps to elongate the tail to one kilometer—fewer than seven hundred.

Elongating a tail from one meter to one kilometer is all very well (and all very absurd), but how do you place the evolution of an eye on the same scale? The problem is that in the case of the eye, lots of things have to go on in lots of different parts, in parallel. Nilsson and Pelger's task was to set up computer models of evolving eyes to answer two questions. The first is essentially the question we posed again and again in the past several pages, but they asked it more systematically, using a computer: Is there a smooth gradient of change, from flat skin to full camera eye, such that every intermediate is an improvement? (Unlike human designers, natural selection can't go downhill—not even if there is a tempting higher hill on the other side of the valley.) Second—the question with which we began this section—how long would the necessary quantity of evolutionary change take?

In their computer models, Nilsson and Pelger made no attempt to simulate the internal workings of cells. They started their story after the invention of a single light-sensitive cell—it does no harm to call it a photocell. It would be nice, in the future, to do another computer model, this time at the level of the inside of the cell, to show how the first living photocell came into being by step-by-step modification of an earlier, more general-purpose cell. But you have to start somewhere, and Nilsson and Pelger started after the invention of the photocell. They worked at the level of tissues: the level of stuff made of cells rather than the level of individual cells. Skin is a tissue, so is the lining of the intestine, so is muscle and liver. Tissues can change in various ways under the influence of random mutation. Sheets of tissue can become larger or smaller in area. They can become thicker or thinner. In the special case of transparent tissues like lens tissue, they can change the refractive index (the light-bending power) of local parts of the tissue.

Computer model of the eye

The beauty of simulating an eye, as distinct from, say, the leg of a running cheetah, is that its efficiency can be easily measured, using the laws of elementary optics. The eye is represented as a two-dimensional cross section, and the computer can easily calculate its visual acuity, or spatial resolution, as a single real number. It would be much harder to come up with an equivalent numerical expression for the efficacy of a cheetah's leg or backbone. Nilsson and Pelger began with a flat retina atop a flat pigment layer and surmounted by a flat, protective transparent layer. The transparent layer was allowed to undergo localized random mutations of its refractive index. They then let the model deform itself at random, constrained only by the requirement that any change must be small and must be an improvement on what went before.

The results were swift and decisive. A trajectory of steadily mounting acuity led unhesitatingly from the flat beginning through a shallow indentation to a steadily deepening cup, as the shape of the model eye deformed itself on the computer screen. The transparent layer thickened to fill the cup and smoothly bulged its outer surface in a curve. And then, almost like a conjuring trick, a portion of this transparent filling condensed into a local, spherical subregion of higher refractive index. Not uniformly higher, but a gradient of refractive index such that the spherical region functioned as an excellent graded-index lens. Graded-index lenses are unfamiliar to human lensmakers but they are common in living eyes. Humans make lenses by grinding glass to a particular shape. We make a compound lens, like the expensive violet-tinted lenses of modern cameras, by mounting several lenses together, but each one of those individual lenses is made of uniform glass through its whole thickness. A graded-index lens, by contrast, has a continuously varying refractive index within its own substance. Typically, it has a high refractive index near the center of the lens. Fish eyes have graded-index lenses. Now it has long been known that, for a graded-index lens, the most aberration-free results are obtained when you achieve a particular theoretical optimum value for the ratio between the focal length of the lens and the radius. This ratio is called Mattiessen's ratio. Nilsson and Pelger's computer model homed in unerringly on Mattiessen's ratio.

And so to the question of how long all this evolutionary change might have taken. In order to answer this, Nilsson and Pelger had to make some assumptions about genetics in natural populations. They needed to feed their model plausible values of quantities such as "heritability." Heritability is a measure of how far variation is governed by heredity. The favored way of measuring it is to see how much monozygotic (that is, "identical") twins resemble each other compared with ordinary twins. One study found the heritability of leg length in male humans to be 77 percent. A heritability of 100 percent would mean that you could measure one identical twin's leg to obtain perfect knowledge of the other twin's leg length, even if the twins were reared apart. A heritability of 0 percent would mean that the legs of monozygotic twins are no more similar to each other than to the legs of random members of a specified population in a given environment. Some other heritabilities measured for humans are 95 percent for head breadth, 85 percent for sitting height, 80 percent for arm length and 79 percent for stature.

Frequency of heritability

Heritabilities are frequently more than 50 percent, and Nilsson and Pelger therefore felt safe in plugging a heritability of 50 percent into their eye model. This was a conservative, or "pessimistic," assumption. Compared with a more realistic assumption of, say, 70 percent, a pessimistic assumption tends to increase their final estimate of the time taken for the eye to evolve. They wanted to err on the side of overestimation because we are intuitively skeptical of short estimates of the time taken to evolve something as complicated as an eye.

For the same reason, they chose pessimistic values for the coefficient of variation (that is, for how much variation there typically is in the population) and the intensity of selection (the amount of survival advantage improved eyesight confers). They even went so far as to assume that any new generation differed in only one part of the eye at a time: simultaneous changes in different parts of the eye, which would have greatly speeded up evolution, were outlawed. But even with these conservative assumptions, the time taken to evolve a fish eye from flat skin was minuscule: fewer than four hundred thousand generations. For the kinds of small animals we are talking about, we can assume one generation per year, so it seems that it would take less than half a million years to evolve a good camera eye.

Heritability is a measure of how far variation is governed by heredity.

In the light of Nilsson and Pelger's results, it is no wonder "the" eye has evolved at least forty times independently around the animal kingdom. There has been enough time for it to evolve from scratch fifteen hundred times in succession within any one lineage. Assuming typical generation lengths for small animals, the time needed for the evolution of the eye, far from stretching credulity with its vastness, turns out to be too short for geologists to measure! It is a geological blink.

Do good by stealth. A key feature of evolution is its gradualness. This is a matter of principle rather than fact. It may or may not be the case that some episodes of evolution take a sudden turn. There may be punctuations of rapid evolution, or even abrupt macromutations—major changes dividing a child from both its parents. There certainly are sudden extinctions—perhaps caused by great natural catastrophes such as comets striking the earth—and these leave vacuums to be filled by rapidly improving understudies, as the mammals replaced the dinosaurs. Evolution is very possibly not, in actual fact, always gradual. But it must be gradual when it is being used to explain the coming into existence of complicated, apparently designed objects, like eyes. For if it is not gradual in these cases, it ceases to have any explanatory power at all. Without gradualness in these cases, we are back to miracle, which is simply a synonym for the total absence of explanation.

The reason eyes and wasp-pollinated orchids impress us so is that they are improbable. The odds against their spontaneously assembling by luck are odds too great to be borne in the real world. Gradual evolution by small steps, each step being lucky but not *too* lucky, is the solution to the riddle. But if it is not gradual, it is no solution to the riddle: it is just a restatement of the riddle.

A key feature of evolution is its gradualness. This is a matter of principle rather than fact.

There will be times when it is hard to think of what the gradual intermediates may have been. These will be challenges to our ingenuity, but if our ingenuity fails, so much the worse for our ingenuity. It does not constitute evidence that there were no gradual intermediates.

2

The Concept of Gradual
Evolution Is Flawed

Michael J. Behe

Michael J. Behe is Associate Professor of Biochemistry at Lehigh University. His field of specialization is molecular biology.

Charles Darwin himself wrote that his theory of evolution would "break down" if it were proven that any complex organ could not have developed over a long period of time in gradual increments. Modern molecular biology has helped prove that there are certain complex organs in both animals and insects that could not have evolved by gradual, successive additions. The concept of *irreducible complexity* helps illustrate that if only one part of a complex organ breaks down, the organ will not work. Such organs could not possibly have evolved over long periods of time.

[C]harles] Darwin knew that his theory of gradual evolution by natural selection carried a heavy burden:

> If it could be demonstrated that any complex organ existed which could not possibly have been formed by numerous, successive, slight modifications, my theory would absolutely break down.[1]

It is safe to say that most of the scientific skepticism about Darwinism in the past century has centered on this requirement. From Mivart's [St. George Mivart, a contemporary critic of Darwin] concern over the incipient stages of new structures to Margulis's [Lynn Margulis, Professor of Biology, University of Massachusetts] dismissal of gradual evolution, critics of Darwin have suspected that his criterion of failure had been met. But how can we be confident? What type of biological system could not be formed by "numerous, successive, slight modifications"?

Well, for starters, a system that is irreducibly complex. By *irreducibly complex* I mean a single system composed of several well-matched, interacting parts that contribute to the basic function, wherein the removal of any one of the parts causes the system to effectively cease functioning. An irreducibly complex system cannot be produced directly (that is, by continuously improving the initial function, which continues to work by the same mechanism) by slight, successive modifications of a precursor system, because any precursor to an irreducibly complex system that is missing a part is by definition nonfunctional. An irreducibly complex biological system, if there is such a thing, would be a powerful challenge to Darwinian evolution. Since natural selection can only choose systems that are already working, then if a biological system cannot be produced gradually it would have to arise as an integrated unit, in one fell swoop, for natural selection to have anything to act on.

Even if a system is irreducibly complex (and thus cannot have been produced directly), however, one can not definitively rule out the possibility of an indirect, circuitous route. As the complexity of an interacting system increases, though, the likelihood of such an indirect route drops precipitously. And as the number of unexplained, irreducibly complex biological systems increases, our confidence that Darwin's criterion of failure has been met skyrockets toward the maximum that science allows.

In the abstract, it might be tempting to imagine that irreducible complexity simply requires multiple simultaneous mutations—that evolution might be far chancier than we thought, but still possible. This is essentially Goldschmidt's [Richard Goldschmidt, mid-20th century geneticist] hopeful-monster theory. Such an appeal to brute luck can never be refuted. Yet it is an empty argument. One may as well say that the world luckily popped into existence yesterday with all the features it now has. Luck is metaphysical speculation; scientific explanations invoke causes. It is almost universally conceded that such sudden events would be irreconcilable with the gradualism Darwin envisioned. Richard Dawkins explains the problem well:

> Evolution is very possibly not, in actual fact, always gradual.
> But it must be gradual when it is being used to explain the
> coming into existence of complicated, apparently designed
> objects, like eyes. For if it is not gradual in these cases, it
> ceases to have any explanatory power at all. Without grad
> ualness in these cases, we are back to miracle, which is sim
> ply a synonym for the total absence of explanation.[2]

The nature of mutation

The reason why this is so rests in the nature of mutation.

In biochemistry, a mutation is a change in DNA. To be inherited, the change must occur in the DNA of a reproductive cell. The simplest mutation occurs when a single nucleotide (nucleotides are the "building blocks" of DNA) in a creature's DNA is switched to a different nucleotide. Alternatively, a single nucleotide can be added or left out when the DNA is copied during cell division. Sometimes, though, a whole region of DNA—thousands or millions of nucleotides—is accidentally deleted or duplicated. That counts as a single mutation, too, because it happens at one time, as a single event. Generally a single mutation can, at best, make only a small change in a creature—even if the change impresses us as a big one. For example, there is a well-known mutation called *antennapedia* that scientists can produce in a laboratory fruit fly: the poor mutant creature has legs growing out of its head instead of antennas. Although that strikes us as a big change, it really isn't. The legs on the head are typical fruit-fly legs, only in a different location.

An analogy may be useful here: Consider a step-by-step list of instructions. A mutation is a change in *one* of the lines of instructions. So instead of saying, "Take a ¼-inch nut," a mutation might say, "Take a ⅜-inch nut." Or instead of "Place the round peg in the round hole," we might get "Place the round peg in the square hole." Or instead of "Attach the seat to the top of the engine," we might get "Attach the seat to the handlebars" (but we could only get this if the nuts and bolts could be attached to the handlebars). What a mutation *cannot* do is change all the instructions in one step—say, to build a fax machine instead of a radio.

Our confidence that Darwin's criterion of failure has been met skyrockets toward the maximum that science allows.

Thus, to go back to the bombardier beetle and the human eye, the question is whether the numerous anatomical changes can be accounted for by many small mutations. The frustrating answer is that *we can't tell.* Both the bombardier beetle's defensive apparatus and the vertebrate eye contain so many molecular components (on the order of tens of thousands of different types of molecules) that listing them—and speculating on the mutations that might have produced them—is currently impossible. Too many of the nuts and bolts (and screws, motor parts, handlebars, and so on) are unaccounted for. For us to debate whether Darwinian evolution could produce such large structures is like nineteenth century scientists debating whether cells could arise spontaneously. Such debates are fruitless because not all the components are known.

We should not, however, lose our perspective over this; other ages have been unable to answer many questions that interested them. Furthermore, because we can't yet evaluate the question of eye evolution or beetle evolution does not mean we can't evaluate Darwinism's claims for any biological structure. When we descend from the level of a whole animal (such as a beetle) or whole organ (such as an eye) to the molecular level, then in many cases we *can* make a judgment on evolution because all of the parts of many discrete molecular systems *are* known.

The mousetrap analogy

Now, let's return to the notion of irreducible complexity. At this point in our discussion *irreducible complexity* is just a term whose power resides mostly in its definition. We must ask how we can recognize an irreducibly complex system. Given the nature of mutation, when can we be sure that a biological system is irreducibly complex?

The first step in determining irreducible complexity is to specify both the function of the system and all system components. An irreducibly complex object will be composed of several parts, all of which contribute to the function. To avoid the problems encountered with extremely complex objects (such as eyes, beetles, or other multicellular biological systems) I will begin with a simple mechanical example: the humble mousetrap.

The function of a mousetrap is to immobilize a mouse so that it can't perform such unfriendly acts as chewing through sacks of flour or electrical cords, or leaving little reminders of its presence in unswept corners. The mousetraps that my family uses consist of a number of parts: (1) a flat wooden platform to act as a base; (2) a metal hammer, which does the actual job of crushing the little mouse; (3) a spring with extended ends to press against the platform and the hammer when the trap is charged; (4) a sensitive catch that releases when slight pressure is applied, and (5) a metal bar that connects to the catch and holds the hammer back when the trap is charged. (There are also assorted staples to hold the system together.)

The second step in determining if a system is irreducibly complex is to ask if all the components are required for the function. In this example, the answer is clearly yes. Suppose that while reading one evening, you hear the patter of little feet in the pantry, and you go to the utility drawer to get a mousetrap. Unfortunately, due to faulty manufacture, the trap is missing one of the parts listed above. Which part could be missing and still allow you to catch a mouse? If the wooden base were gone, there would be no platform for attaching the other components. If the hammer were gone, the mouse could dance all night on the platform without becoming pinned to the wooden base. If there were no spring, the hammer and platform would jangle loosely, and again the rodent would be unimpeded. If there were no catch or metal holding bar, then the spring would snap the hammer shut as soon as you let go of it; in order to use a trap like that you would have to chase the mouse around while holding the trap open.

To be a precursor in Darwin's sense we must show that a motorcycle can be built from "numerous, successive, slight modifications" to a bicycle.

To feel the full force of the conclusion that a system is irreducibly complex and therefore has no functional precursors, we need to distinguish between a *physical* precursor and a *conceptual* precursor. The trap described above is not the only system that can immobilize a mouse. On other occasions my family has used a glue trap. In theory, at least, one can use a box propped open with a stick that could be tripped. Or one can simply shoot the mouse with a BB gun. These are not physical precursors to the standard mousetrap, however, since they cannot be transformed, step by Darwinian step, into a trap with a base, hammer, spring, catch, and holding bar.

To clarify the point, consider this sequence: skateboard, toy wagon, bicycle, motorcycle, automobile, airplane, jet plane, space shuttle. It seems like a natural progression, both because it is a list of objects that all can be used for transportation and also because they are lined up in order of complexity. They can be conceptually connected and blended together into a single continuum. But is, say, a bicycle a physical (and potentially

Darwinian) precursor of a motorcycle? No. It is only a *conceptual* precursor. No motorcycle in history, not even the first, was made simply by modifying a bicycle in a stepwise fashion. It might easily be the case that a teenager on a Saturday afternoon could take an old bicycle, an old lawnmower engine, and some spare parts and (with a couple of hours of effort) build himself a functioning motorcycle. But this only shows that humans can design irreducibly complex systems, which we knew already. To be a precursor in Darwin's sense we must show that a motorcycle can be built from "numerous, successive, slight modifications" to a bicycle.

The evolution of a motorcycle

So let us attempt to evolve a bicycle into a motorcycle by the gradual accumulation of mutations. Suppose that a factory produced bicycles, but that occasionally there was a mistake in manufacture. Let us further suppose that if the mistake led to an improvement in the bicycle, then the friends and neighbors of the lucky buyer would demand similar bikes, and the factory would retool to make the mutation a permanent feature. So, like biological mutations, successful mechanical mutations would reproduce and spread. If we are to keep our analogy relevant to biology, however, each change can only be a slight modification, duplication, or rearrangement of a preexisting component, and the change must improve the function of the bicycle. So if the factory mistakenly increased the size of a nut or decreased the diameter of a bolt, or added an extra wheel onto the front axle or left off the rear tire, or put a pedal on the handlebars or added extra spokes, and if any of these slight changes improved the bike ride, then the improvement would immediately be noticed by the buying public and the mutated bikes would, in true Darwinian fashion, dominate the market.

Given these conditions, can we evolve a bicycle into a motorcycle? We can move in the right direction by making the seat more comfortable in small steps, the wheels bigger, and even (assuming our customers prefer the "biker" look) imitating the overall shape in various ways. But a motorcycle depends on a source of fuel, and a bicycle has nothing that can be slightly modified to become a gasoline tank. And what part of the bicycle could be duplicated to begin building a motor? Even if a lucky accident brought a lawnmower engine from a neighboring factory into the bicycle factory, the motor would have to be mounted on the bike and be connected in the right way to the drive chain. How could this be done step-by-step from bicycle parts? A factory that made bicycles simply could not produce a motorcycle by natural selection acting on variation—by "numerous, successive, slight modifications"—and in fact there is no example in history of a complex change in a product occurring in this manner.

A bicycle thus may be a conceptual precursor to a motorcycle, but it is not a physical one. Darwinian evolution requires physical precursors.

Minimal function

So far we have examined the question of irreducible complexity as a challenge to step-by-step evolution. But there is another difficulty for Darwin. My previous list of factors that render a mousetrap irreducibly complex was actually much too generous, because almost any device with the five components of a standard mousetrap will nonetheless fail to function. If the base were made out of paper, for example, the trap would fall apart. If the hammer were too heavy, it would break the spring. If the spring were too loose, it would not move the hammer. If the holding bar were too short, it would not reach the catch. If the catch were too large, it would not release at the proper time. A simple list of components of a mousetrap is necessary, but not sufficient, to make a functioning mousetrap.

In order to be a candidate for natural selection a system must have *minimal function:* the ability to accomplish a task in physically realistic circumstances. A mousetrap made of unsuitable materials would not meet the criterion of minimal function, but even complex machines that do what they are supposed to do may not be of much use. To illustrate, suppose that the world's first outboard motor had been designed and was being marketed. The motor functioned smoothly—burning gasoline at a controlled rate, transmitting the force along an axle, and turning the propeller—but the propeller rotated at only one revolution per hour. This is an impressive technological feat; after all, burning gasoline in a can next to a propeller doesn't turn it at all. Nonetheless, few people would purchase such a machine, because it fails to perform at a level suitable for its purpose.

Irreducibly complex systems are nasty roadblocks for Darwinian evolution.

Performance can be unsuitable for either of two reasons. The first reason is that the machine does not get the job done. A couple fishing in the middle of a lake in a boat with a slow-turning propeller would not get to the dock: random currents of the water and wind would knock their boat off course. The second reason that performance might be unsuitable is if it is less efficient than can be achieved with simpler means. No one would use an inefficient, outboard motor if they could do just as well or better with a sail.

Unlike irreducible complexity (where we can enumerate discrete parts), minimal function is sometimes hard to define. If one revolution per hour is insufficient for an outboard motor, how about a hundred? Or a thousand? Nonetheless, minimal function is critical in the evolution of biological structures. For example, what is the minimum amount of hydroquinone that a predator can taste? How much of a rise in the temperature of the solution will it notice? If the predator didn't notice a tiny bit of hydroquinone or a small change in temperature, then our Dawkinsesque tale of the bombardier beetle's evolution can be filed alongside the story of the cow jumping over the moon. Irreducibly complex systems are nasty roadblocks for Darwinian evolution; the need for minimal function greatly exacerbates the dilemma.

Nuts and bolts

Biochemistry has demonstrated that any biological apparatus involving more than one cell (such as an organ or a tissue) is necessarily an intricate web of many different, identifiable systems of horrendous complexity. The "simplest" self-sufficient, replicating cell has the capacity to produce thousands of different proteins and other molecules, at different times and under variable conditions. Synthesis, degradation, energy generation, replication, maintenance of cell architecture, mobility, regulation, repair, communication—all of these functions take place in virtually every cell, and each function itself requires the interaction of numerous parts. Because each cell is such an interwoven meshwork of systems, we would be repeating the mistake of Francis Hitching by asking if multicellular structures could have evolved in step-by-step Darwinian fashion. That would be like asking not whether a bicycle could evolve into a motorcycle, but whether a bicycle factory could evolve into a motorcycle factory! Evolution does not take place on the factory level; it takes place on the nut-and-bolt level.

The arguments of Dawkins and [science writer] Hitching fail because they never discuss what is contained in the systems over which they are arguing. Not only is the eye exceedingly complex, but the "light-sensitive spot" with which Dawkins begins his case is itself a multicelled organ, each of whose cells makes the complexity of a motorcycle or television set look paltry in comparison. Not only does the defensive apparatus of the bombardier beetle depend on a number of interacting components, but the cells that produce hydroquinone and hydrogen peroxide depend on a very large number of components to do so; the cells that secrete catalase are very complex; and the sphincter muscle separating the collection vesicle from the explosion chamber is a system of systems. Because of this, Hitching's arguments about the splendid complexity of the bombardier beetle are easily blurred into irrelevance, and Dawkins's reply satisfies us only until we ask for more details.

It is the requirements of the structure-function relationship itself that block Darwinian-style evolution.

In contrast to biological organs, the analysis of simple mechanical objects is relatively straightforward. We showed in short order that a mousetrap is irreducibly complex, and so we can conclude what we already knew—that a mousetrap is made as an intact system. We already knew that a motorcycle was not unconsciously produced by small, successive improvements to a bicycle, and a quick analysis shows us that it is impossible to do so. Mechanical objects can't reproduce and mutate like biological systems, but hypothesizing comparable events at an imaginary factory shows that mutation and reproduction are not the main barriers to evolution of mechanical objects. It is the requirements of the structure-function relationship itself that block Darwinian-style evolution.

Machines are relatively easy to analyze because both their function and all of their parts, each nut and bolt, are known and can be listed. It is then simple to see if any given part is required for the function of the system. If a system requires several closely matched parts to function then it is irreducibly complex, and we can conclude that it was produced as an integrated unit. In principle, biological systems can also be analyzed in this manner, but only if all the parts of the system can be enumerated and a function recognized.

Notes

1. Darwin, C. (1872) *Origin of Species*, 6th ed. (1988), New York University Press, New York, p. 154.

2. Dawkins, R. (1995) *River out of Eden*, Basic Books, New York, p. 83.

3

"Creationism" Should Not Be Taught in Science Classrooms

National Academy of Sciences

The National Academy of Sciences is a private, nonprofit, self-perpetuating society of distinguished scholars engaged in scientific and engineering research, dedicated to the furtherance of science and technology and to their use for the general welfare.

Scientific observations have confirmed many hypotheses related to the origin and age of the universe and the earth. Even questions involving the origins of life have graduated from the uncertainty of "could" life have originated from non-living components to the more confident "how" did life originate. The beliefs held by divine creationists, namely that the earth is no more than 10,000 years old and/or that living things resulted from supernatural intervention are inconsistent with contemporary scientific discoveries. Nor can they be substantiated scientifically. For these and other reasons, creationism should not be taught in science classrooms.

The term "evolution" usually refers to the biological evolution of living things. But the processes by which planets, stars, galaxies, and the universe form and change over time are also types of "evolution." In all of these cases there is change over time, although the processes involved are quite different.

In the late 1920s the American astronomer Edwin Hubble made a very interesting and important discovery. Hubble made observations that he interpreted as showing that distant stars and galaxies are receding from Earth in every direction. Moreover, the velocities of recession increase in proportion with distance, a discovery that has been confirmed by numerous and repeated measurements since Hubble's time. The implication of these findings is that the universe is expanding.

Hubble's hypothesis of an expanding universe leads to certain deductions. One is that the universe was more condensed at a previous time. From this deduction came the suggestion that all the currently observed matter and energy in the universe were initially condensed in a very small and infinitely hot mass. A huge explosion, known as the Big Bang, then sent matter and energy expanding in all directions.

The Big Bang hypothesis

This Big Bang hypothesis led to more testable deductions. One such deduction was that the temperature in deep space today should be several degrees above absolute zero. Observations showed this deduction to be correct. In fact, the Cosmic Microwave Background Explorer (COBE) satellite launched in 1991 confirmed that the background radiation field has exactly the spectrum predicted by a Big Bang origin for the universe.

As the universe expanded, according to current scientific understanding, matter collected into clouds that began to condense and rotate, forming the forerunners of galaxies. Within galaxies, including our own Milky Way galaxy, changes in pressure caused gas and dust to form distinct clouds. In some of these clouds, where there was sufficient mass and the right forces, gravitational attraction caused the cloud to collapse. If the mass of material in the cloud was sufficiently compressed, nuclear reactions began and a star was born.

Some proportion of stars, including our sun, formed in the middle of a flattened spinning disk of material. In the case of our sun, the gas and dust within this disk collided and aggregated into small grains, and the grains formed into larger bodies called planetesimals ("very small planets"), some of which reached diameters of several hundred kilometers. In successive stages these planetesimals coalesced into the nine planets and their numerous satellites. The rocky planets, including Earth, were near the sun, and the gaseous planets were in more distant orbits.

The origins of life cannot be dated as precisely, but there is evidence that bacteria-like organisms lived on Earth 3.5 billion years ago, and they may have existed even earlier.

The ages of the universe, our galaxy, the solar system, and Earth can be estimated using modern scientific methods. The age of the universe can be derived from the observed relationship between the velocities of and the distances separating the galaxies. The velocities of distant galaxies can be measured very accurately, but the measurement of distances is more uncertain. Over the past few decades, measurements of the Hubble expansion have led to estimated ages for the universe of between 7 billion and 20 billion years, with the most recent and best measurements within the range of 10 billion to 15 billion years.

The age of the Milky Way galaxy has been calculated in two ways. One involves studying the observed stages of evolution of different-sized stars in globular clusters. Globular clusters occur in a faint halo surrounding the center of the Galaxy, with each cluster containing from a hundred thousand to a million stars. The very low amounts of elements heavier than hydrogen and helium in these stars indicate that they must have formed early in the history of the Galaxy, before large amounts of heavy elements were created inside the initial generations of stars and later distributed into the interstellar medium through supernova explosions (the Big Bang itself created primarily hydrogen and helium atoms). Estimates of the ages of the stars in globular clusters fall within the range of 11 billion to 16 billion years.

A second method for estimating the age of our galaxy is based on the present abundances of several long-lived radioactive elements in the solar system. Their abundances are set by their rates of production and distribution through exploding supernovas. According to these calculations, the age of our galaxy is between 9 billion and 16 billion years. Thus, both ways of estimating the age of the Milky Way galaxy agree with each other, and they also are consistent with the independently derived estimate for the age of the universe.

Radioactive dating techniques

Radioactive elements occurring naturally in rocks and minerals also provide a means of estimating the age of the solar system and Earth. Several of these elements decay with half lives between 700 million and more than 100 billion years (the half life of an element is the time it takes for half of the element to decay radioactively into another element). Using these time-keepers, it is calculated that meteorites, which are fragments of asteroids, formed between 4.53 billion and 4.58 billion years ago (asteroids are small "planetoids" that revolve around the sun and are remnants of the solar nebula that gave rise to the sun and planets). The same radioactive time-keepers applied to the three oldest lunar samples returned to Earth by the Apollo astronauts yield ages between 4.4 billion and 4.5 billion years, providing minimum estimates for the time since the formation of the moon.

The oldest known rocks on Earth occur in northwestern Canada (3.96 billion years), but well-studied rocks nearly as old are also found in other parts of the world. In Western Australia, zircon crystals encased within younger rocks have ages as old as 4.3 billion years, making these tiny crystals the oldest materials so far found on Earth.

The best estimates of Earth's age are obtained by calculating the time required for development of the observed lead isotopes in Earth's oldest lead ores. These estimates yield 4.54 billion years as the age of Earth and of meteorites, and hence of the solar system.

The origins of life cannot be dated as precisely, but there is evidence that bacteria-like organisms lived on Earth 3.5 billion years ago, and they may have existed even earlier, when the first solid crust formed, almost 4 billion years ago. These early organisms must have been simpler than the organisms living today. Furthermore, before the earliest organisms there must have been structures that one would not call "alive" but that are now components of living things. Today, all living organisms store and transmit hereditary information using two kinds of molecules: DNA and RNA. Each of these molecules is in turn composed of four kinds of subunits known as nucleotides. The sequences of nucleotides in particular lengths of DNA or RNA, known as genes, direct the construction of molecules known as proteins, which in turn catalyze biochemical reactions, provide structural components for organisms, and perform many of the other functions on which life depends. Proteins consist of chains of subunits known as amino acids. The sequence of nucleotides in DNA and RNA therefore determines the sequence of amino acids in proteins; this is a central mechanism in all of biology.

Experiments conducted under conditions intended to resemble those present on primitive Earth have resulted in the production of some of the chemical components of proteins, DNA, and RNA. Some of these molecules also have been detected in meteorites from outer space and in interstellar space by astronomers using radio-telescopes. Scientists have concluded that the "building blocks of life" could have been available early in Earth's history.

"Autocatalytic" molecules

An important new research avenue has opened with the discovery that certain molecules made of RNA, called ribozymes, can act as catalysts in modern cells. It previously had been thought that only proteins could serve as the catalysts required to carry out specific biochemical functions. Thus, in the early prebiotic world, RNA molecules could have been "autocatalytic"—that is, they could have replicated themselves well before there were any protein catalysts (called enzymes). Laboratory experiments demonstrate that replicating autocatalytic RNA molecules undergo spontaneous changes and that the variants of RNA molecules with the greatest autocatalytic activity come to prevail in their environments. Some scientists favor the hypothesis that there was an early "RNA world," and they are testing models that lead from RNA to the synthesis of simple DNA and protein molecules. These assemblages of molecules eventually could have become packaged within membranes, thus making up "protocells"—early versions of very simple cells.

For those who are studying the origin of life, the question is no longer whether life could have originated by chemical processes involving non-biological components. The question instead has become which of many pathways might have been followed to produce the first cells.

There are no valid scientific data or calculations to substantiate the belief that Earth was created just a few thousand years ago.

Will we ever be able to identify the path of chemical evolution that succeeded in initiating life on Earth? Scientists are designing experiments and speculating about how early Earth could have provided a hospitable site for the segregation of molecules in units that might have been the first living systems. The recent speculation includes the possibility that the first living cells might have arisen on Mars, seeding Earth via the many meteorites that are known to travel from Mars to our planet.

Of course, even if a living cell were to be made in the laboratory, it would not prove that nature followed the same pathway billions of years ago. But it is the job of science to provide plausible natural explanations for natural phenomena. The study of the origin of life is a very active research area in which important progress is being made, although the consensus among scientists is that none of the current hypotheses has thus far been confirmed. The history of science shows that seemingly intractable problems like this one may become amenable to solution later, as a result of advances in theory, instrumentation, or the discovery of new facts.

Creationist views of the origin of the universe, earth, and life

Many religious persons, including many scientists, hold that God created the universe and the various processes driving physical and biological evolution and that these processes then resulted in the creation of galaxies, our solar system, and life on Earth. This belief, which sometimes is termed "theistic evolution," is not in disagreement with scientific explanations of evolution. Indeed, it reflects the remarkable and inspiring character of the physical universe revealed by cosmology, paleontology, molecular biology, and many other scientific disciplines.

The advocates of "creation science" hold a variety of viewpoints. Some claim that Earth and the universe are relatively young, perhaps only 6,000 to 10,000 years old. These individuals often believe that the present physical form of Earth can be explained by "catastrophism," including a worldwide flood, and that all living things (including humans) were created miraculously, essentially in the forms we now find them.

No body of beliefs that has its origin in doctrinal material rather than scientific observation, interpretation, and experimentation should be admissible as science in any science course.

Other advocates of creation science are willing to accept that Earth, the planets, and the stars may have existed for millions of years. But they argue that the various types of organisms, and especially humans, could only have come about with supernatural intervention, because they show "intelligent design."

In this booklet, both these "Young Earth" and "Old Earth" views are referred to as "creationism" or "special creation."

There are no valid scientific data or calculations to substantiate the belief that Earth was created just a few thousand years ago. This document has summarized the vast amount of evidence for the great age of the universe, our galaxy, the solar system, and Earth from astronomy, astrophysics, nuclear physics, geology, geochemistry, and geophysics. Independent scientific methods consistently give an age for Earth and the solar system of about 5 billion years, and an age for our galaxy and the universe that is two to three times greater. These conclusions make the origin of the universe as a whole intelligible, lend coherence to many different branches of science, and form the core conclusions of a remarkable body of knowledge about the origins and behavior of the physical world.

Nor is there any evidence that the entire geological record, with its orderly succession of fossils, is the product of a single universal flood that occurred a few thousand years ago, lasted a little longer than a year, and covered the highest mountains to a depth of several meters. On the contrary, intertidal and terrestrial deposits demonstrate that at no recorded time in the past has the entire planet been under water. Moreover, a universal flood of sufficient magnitude to form the sedimentary rocks seen today, which together are many kilometers thick, would require a volume of water far greater than has ever existed on and in Earth, at least since the formation of the first known solid crust about 4 billion years ago. The belief that Earth's sediments, with their fossils, were deposited in an orderly sequence in a year's time defies all geological observations and physical principles concerning sedimentation rates and possible quantities of suspended solid matter.

Geological studies

Geologists have constructed a detailed history of sediment deposition that links particular bodies of rock in the crust of Earth to particular environments and processes. If petroleum geologists could find more oil and gas by interpreting the record of sedimentary rocks as having resulted from a single flood, they would certainly favor the idea of such a flood, but they do not. Instead, these practical workers agree with academic geologists about the nature of depositional environments and geological time. Petroleum geologists have been pioneers in the recognition of fossil deposits that were formed over millions of years in such environments as meandering rivers, deltas, sandy barrier beaches, and coral reefs.

The example of petroleum geology demonstrates one of the great strengths of science. By using knowledge of the natural world to predict the consequences of our actions, science makes it possible to solve problems and create opportunities using technology. The detailed knowledge required to sustain our civilization could only have been derived through scientific investigation.

The arguments of creationists are not driven by evidence that can be observed in the natural world. Special creation or supernatural intervention is not subjectable to meaningful tests, which require predicting plausible results and then checking these results through observation and experimentation. Indeed, claims of "special creation" reverse the scientific process. The explanation is seen as unalterable, and evidence is sought only to support a particular conclusion by whatever means possible. . . .

Science and creationism

Science is not the only way of acquiring knowledge about ourselves and the world around us. Humans gain understanding in many other ways, such as through literature, the arts, philosophical reflection, and religious experience. Scientific knowledge may enrich aesthetic and moral perceptions, but these subjects extend beyond science's realm, which is to obtain a better understanding of the natural world.

The claim that equity demands balanced treatment of evolutionary theory and special creation in science classrooms reflects a misunderstanding of what science is and how it is conducted. Scientific investigators seek to understand natural phenomena by observation and experimentation. Scientific interpretations of facts and the explanations that account for them therefore must be testable by observation and experimentation.

Creationism, intelligent design, and other claims of supernatural intervention in the origin of life or of species are not science because they are not testable by the methods of science. These claims subordinate observed data to statements based on authority, revelation, or religious belief. Documentation offered in support of these claims is typically limited to the special publications of their advocates. These publications do not offer hypotheses subject to change in light of new data, new interpretations, or demonstration of error. This contrasts with science, where any hypothesis or theory always remains subject to the possibility of rejection or modification in the light of new knowledge.

No body of beliefs that has its origin in doctrinal material rather than scientific observation, interpretation, and experimentation should be admissible as science in any science course. Incorporating the teaching of such doctrines into a science curriculum compromises the objectives of public education. Science has been greatly successful at explaining natural processes, and this has led not only to increased understanding of the universe but also to major improvements in technology and public health and welfare. The growing role that science plays in modern life requires that science, and not religion, be taught in science classes.

4

"Scientific Creationism" Should Be Taught in Science Classrooms

Duane T. Gish

Duane T. Gish received a B.S. degree in chemistry from the University of California at Los Angeles, and a Ph.D. in biochemistry from the University of California at Berkeley. He is the author of numerous articles and several books and a worldwide lecturer on the subject of the scientific evidence for creation. Dr. Gish is one of the founders and a board member of the Creation Research Society, St. Joseph, Missouri.

Within the domain of empirical science, creation scientists and evolutionary scientists operate in a similar way. Both assume that events in the physical world today mirror the past and foreshadow the future. But neither creation nor evolution may be referred to as scientific theory since neither can offer eyewitness evidence of what happened in the past. Both are ultimately based upon inferences derived from circumstantial evidence. As such, they remain on an equal footing and should receive equal time in public classrooms in the United States.

Science is our attempt to observe, understand and explain the operation of the universe and of the living things found here on planet Earth. Since a scientific theory, by definition, must be testable by repeatable observations and must be capable of being falsified if indeed it were false, a scientific theory can only attempt to explain processes and events that are presently occurring repeatedly within our observations. Theories about history, although interesting and often fruitful, are not scientific theories, even though they may be related to other theories which do fulfill the criteria of a scientific theory. While operating within the domain of empirical science, creation scientists function in exactly the same manner as evolution scientists, assuming that what they see happening today happened in the past and will happen in the same way in the future. Science is empirical, and thus this is the only way a scientist can operate.

Excerpted from *Teaching Creation Science in Public Schools,* by Duane T. Gish. Copyright © 1995 by Institute for Creation Research. Reprinted with permission from Institute for Creation Research.

The nature of theories on origins

On the other hand, the theory of creation and the theory of evolution are attempts to explain the origin of the universe and of its inhabitants. There were no human observers to the origin of the universe, the origin of life, or as a matter of fact, to the origin of a single living species. These events were unique historical events which have occurred only once. Thus, no one has ever seen anything created, nor has anyone ever seen a fish evolve into an amphibian nor an ape evolve into man. Furthermore, it is impossible to go into the laboratory and test any theory on how a fish may have changed into an amphibian or how an ape-like creature may have evolved into man. The changes we see occurring today are mere fluctuations in populations which result neither in an increase in complexity nor significant change. Therefore, neither creation nor evolution is a scientific theory. Creation and evolution are inferences based on circumstantial evidence.

The notion . . . that evolution is a scientific theory while creation is nothing more than religious mysticism is blatantly false.

Thus the notion, repeated incessantly by evolutionists, that evolution is a scientific theory while creation is nothing more than religious mysticism is blatantly false. This is being recognized more and more today, even by evolutionists themselves. Karl Popper, one of the world's leading philosophers of science, has stated that evolution is not a scientific theory but is a metaphysical research program.[1] Birch and Ehrlich state that:

> Our theory of evolution has become . . . one which cannot be refuted by any possible observation. Every conceivable observation can be fitted into it. It is thus "outside of empirical science" but not necessarily false. No one can think of ways in which to test it. Ideas, either without basis or based on a few laboratory experiments carried out in extremely simplified systems have attained currency far beyond their validity. They have become part of an evolutionary dogma accepted by most of us as part of our training.[2]

Green and Goldberger, with reference to theories on the origin of life, have said that:

> . . . the macromolecule-to-cell transition is a jump of fantastic dimensions, which lies beyond the range of testable hypothesis. In this area all is conjecture.[3]

It seems obvious that a theory that is outside of empirical science because no one can think of ways to test it, or a theory that lies beyond the range of testable hypothesis, cannot qualify as a scientific theory. Any suggestion that these challenges to the status of evolution as a scientific theory are exceptions lifted out of the evolutionary literature by creation scientists can be refuted by a thorough search of that literature. Even Futuyma, one of those who has recently written a book attempting to refute creation, states in that book that:

> Two major kinds of arguments about evolutionary theory occur within scientific circles. There are philosophical arguments about whether or not evolutionary theory qualifies as a scientific theory, and substantive arguments about the details of the theory and their adequacy to explain observed phenomena. . . . A secondary issue then arises: Is the hypothesis of natural selection falsifiable or is it a tautology? . . . The claim that natural selection is a tautology is periodically made in the scientific literature itself. . . ."[4]

It is evident that the major challenge to the status of evolution as a scientific theory comes from within the evolutionary establishment itself, not from creation scientists.

Creation and evolution are thus theoretical inferences about history. Even though neither qualifies, strictly speaking, as a scientific theory, each possesses scientific character, since each attempts to correlate and explain scientific data. Creation and evolution are best characterized as explanatory scientific models which are employed to correlate and explain data related to origins. The terms "creation theory," "evolution theory," "creation science" and "evolution science" are appropriate as long as it is clear that the use of such terms denote certain inferences about the history of origins which employ scientific data rather than referring to testable and potentially falsifiable scientific theories. Since neither is a scientific theory and each seeks to explain the same scientific data related to origins, it is not only incorrect but arrogant and self-serving to declare that evolution is science while creation is mere religion. Creation is in every sense as scientific as evolution.

The relationship of theories on origins to philosophy and religion

No theory on origins can be devoid of philosophical and religious implications. Creation implies the existence of a Creator (a person or persons, a force, an intelligence, or whatever one may wish to impute). The creation scientist assumes that the natural universe is the product of the design, purpose and direct volitional acts of a Creator. Science can tell us nothing about who the Creator is, why the universe was created, or anything about the relationship of the things created to the Creator. Creation scientists have no intention of introducing religious literature into science classes or science textbooks in the public schools of the United States. It is thus absolutely untrue to say that creation scientists are seeking to introduce Biblical creation into the public schools. Their desire is that the subject of origins be taught in a philosophically and religiously neutral manner, as required by the U.S. Constitution.

On the other hand, evolution is a non-theistic theory of origins which by definition excludes the intervention of an outside agency of any kind. Evolutionists believe that by employing natural laws and processes *plus nothing* it is possible to explain the origin of the universe and of all that it contains. This involves the acceptance of a particular philosophical or metaphysical world view and is thus basically religious in nature. The fact that creation and evolution involve fundamentally different world views has been frankly admitted by some evolutionists. For example, Lewontin has said:

> Yet, whatever our understanding of the social struggle that gives rise to creationism, whatever the desire to reconcile science and religion may be, there is no escape from the fundamental contradiction between evolution and creationism. They are irreconcilable world views.[5]

Thus, Lewontin characterizes creation and evolution as *irreconcilable world views,* and as such each involves commitment to irreconcilable philosophical and religious positions. This does not imply that all evolutionists are atheists or agnostics, nor does it imply that all creationists are Bible-believing fundamentalists.

Teaching evolution science exclusively . . . encourages belief in a non-theistic, and in fact, an essentially atheistic, world view.

While it is true that teaching creation science exclusively would encourage belief in a theistic world-view, it is equally true that teaching evolution science exclusively (as is essentially the case in the U.S. today) encourages belief in a non-theistic, and in fact, an essentially atheistic, world view. Indoctrinating our young people in evolutionism tends to convince them that they are hardly more than a mechanistic product of a mindless universe, that there is no God, that there is no one to whom they are responsible. Thus, Julian Huxley asserted that:

> Darwinism removed the whole idea of God as the creator of organisms from the sphere of rational discussion . . . we can dismiss entirely all ideas of a supernatural overriding mind being responsible for the evolutionary process.[6]

In their literature, humanists have proclaimed that humanism is a "non-theistic religion." They quote Sir Julian Huxley as stating:

> I use the word "Humanist" to mean someone who believes that man is just as much a natural phenomenon as an animal or plant; that his body, mind and soul were not supernaturally created but are products of evolution. . . .[7]

In his review of George Gaylord Simpson's book *Life of the Past,*[8] Huxley says:

> And he concludes the book with a splendid assertion of the evolutionists' view of man. Man, he writes, "stands alone in the universe, a unique product of a long, unconscious, impersonal, material process. . . . He can and must decide and manage his own destiny."[9]

In his eulogy to Theodosius Dobzhansky, one of the world's leading evolutionists until his death, Ayala wrote that:

. . . Dobzhansky believed and propounded that the implications of biological evolution reach much beyond biology into philosophy, sociology, and even socio-political issues. The place of biological evolution in human thought was, according to Dobzhansky, best expressed in a passage he often quoted from Pierre Teilhard de Chardin: "(Evolution) is a general postulate to which all theories, all hypotheses, all systems must henceforward bow and which they must satisfy in order to be thinkable and true. Evolution is a light which illuminates all facts, a trajectory which all lines of thought must follow—this is what evolution is."[10]

The above statement is as heavily saturated with religion as any assertion could be, and yet it is quoted approvingly by Ayala and Dobzhansky, two of the main architects of the neo-Darwinian theory of evolution.

No professionally trained teacher should thus hesitate to teach the scientific evidence that supports creation as an alternative to evolution.

It is no wonder that Marjorie Grene, a leading philosopher and historian of science, has stated that:

It is as a *religion of science* that Darwinism chiefly held, and holds men's minds. The derivation of life, of man, of man's deepest hopes and highest achievements, from the external and indirect determination of small chance errors, appears as the very keystone of the naturalistic universe. . . . Today the tables are turned. The modified, but still characteristically Darwinian theory has itself become an orthodoxy preached by its adherents with religious fervor, and doubted, they feel, only by a few muddlers imperfect in scientific faith.[11]

Birch and Ehrlich have used the term "evolutionary dogma," Grene has referred to Darwinism as a "religion of science," an "orthodoxy preached by its adherents with religious fervor," and Dobzhansky and Teilhard de Chardin proclaim that all theories, hypotheses, and systems must bow before evolution in order to be thinkable and true. One could easily search the evolutionary literature to find many other examples that reveal the religious nature of the evolutionary world view. *It can thus be stated unequivocally that evolution is as religious as creation, and conversely, that creation is as scientific as evolution.*

Creation and evolution are the only valid alternative theories of origins

Evolutionists often assert that creationists have constructed a false dichotomy between creation and evolution, that there are actually many theories of origins. While it is true that there are several sub-models within the general creation model, just as there are several sub-models within the general evolution model, all theories of origins can be fitted within these two general theories. Thus, Futuyma, an evolutionist as we have noted earlier, states:

> Creation and Evolution, between them, exhaust the possible explanations for the origin of living things. Organisms either appeared on the earth fully developed or they did not. If they did not, they must have developed from preexisting species by some process of modification. If they did appear in a fully developed state, they must indeed have been created by some omnipotent intelligence.[12]

No professionally trained teacher should thus hesitate to teach the scientific evidence that supports creation as an alternative to evolution. This is recognized by Alexander, who stated that:

> No teacher should be dismayed at efforts to present creation as an alternative to evolution in biology courses; indeed at this moment creation is the only alternative to evolution. Not only is this worth mentioning, but a comparison of the two alternatives can be an excellent exercise in logic and reason. Our primary goal as educators should be to teach students to think . . . . Creation and evolution in some respects imply backgrounds about as different as one can imagine. In the sense that creation is an alternative to evolution for any specific question, a case against creation is a case for evolution, and *vice versa*.[13]

In a sense, both creation and evolution are based on axioms, assertions that are assumed to be true and which have predictable consequences. In his conclusion to a paper in which he gives an axiomatic interpretation of the neo–Darwinian theory of evolution, C. Leon Harris states:

> First, the axiomatic nature of the neo–Darwinian theory places the debate between evolutionists and creationists in a new perspective. Evolutionists have often challenged creationists to provide experimental proof that species have been fashioned *de novo*. Creationists have often demanded that evolutionists show how chance mutations can lead to adaptability, or to explain why natural selection has favored some species but not others with special adaptations, or why natural selection allows apparently detrimental organs to persist. We may now recognize that neither challenge is fair. If the neo–Darwinian theory is axiomatic, it is not valid for creationists to demand proof of the axioms, and it is not valid for evolutionists to dismiss special creation as unproved so long as it is stated as an axiom.[14]

That belief in creation and evolution is *exactly parallel* was frankly stated by the prominent British biologist and evolutionist, L. Harrison Matthews. Matthews thus states:

> . . . The fact of evolution is the backbone of biology, and bi-

ology is thus in the peculiar position of being a science founded on an unproved theory—is it then a science or a faith? Belief in the theory of evolution is thus exactly parallel to belief in special creation—both are concepts which believers know to be true but neither, up to the present, has been capable of proof.[15]

Teaching both theories of origins is an educational imperative

Thus, since creation is as scientific as evolution, and evolution is as religious as creation; since creation and evolution between them exhaust the possible explanations for origins; a comparison of the two alternatives can be excellent exercises in logic and reason; no theory in science should be allowed to freeze into dogma, immune from the challenge of alternative theories; academic and religious freedoms are guaranteed by the United States Constitution; public schools are supported by the taxes derived from all citizens; therefore, in the public schools in the United States, the scientific evidences which support creation should be taught along with the scientific evidences which support evolution in a philosophically neutral manner devoid of references to any religious literature.

Notes

1. Karl Popper, in *The Philosphy of Karl Popper*, ed. P.A. Schilpp, Vol. 1 (La Salle, IL: Open Court), pp. 133–43.

2. L.C. Birch and P.R. Ehrlich, *Nature* 214 (1967): 369.

3. D.E. Green and R.F. Goldberger, *Molecular Insights into the Living Process* (New York: Academic Press, 1967), p. 407.

4. D.J. Futuyma, *Science on Trial* (New York: Pantheon Books, 1983), p. 171.

5. R. Lewontin, in the Introduction to *Scientists Confront Creationism*, ed. L.R. Godfrey (New York: W.W. Norton and Co., 1983), p. xxvi.

6. J. Huxley, in *Issues in Evolution*, ed. S. Tax (Chicago: University of Chicago Press, 1960), p. 45.

7. "What is Humanism?" Humanist Community of San Jose (San Jose, CA 95106).

8. G.G. Simpson, *Life of the Past* (New Haven, Conn.: Yale University Press, 1953), p. 157.

9. J. Huxley, *Scientific American*, 189 (1953): 90.

10. F.J. Ayala, J. Heredity 63 (1977): 3.

11. M. Grene, *Encounter* (Nov. 1959), pp. 48–50.

12. D.J. Futuyma, *Science on Trial*, p. 197.

13. R.D. Alexander, in *Evolution versus Creationism: The Public Education Controversy* (Phoenix: Oryx Press, 1983), p. 91.

14. C.L. Harris, *Perspectives in Biology and Medicine* (Winter 1975), p. 179.

15. L.H. Matthews, Introduction to *The Origin of Species*, C. Darwin (Reprint. London: J.M. Dent and Sons, Ltd., 1971), p. x.

5

Physical Laws Support Creationism

Ker C. Thomson

Ker C. Thomson is a former Director of the US Air Force Terrestrial Sciences Laboratory. He holds a B.A. in Physics and Geology from the University of British Columbia and DSc in Geophysics from the Colorado School of Mines. Thomson served as Professor of Geophysics at Baylor University and Professor of Science at Bryan College. He has published numerous technical papers in the area of geophysics and seismology.

The Second Law of Thermodynamics states that all things in the Universe are undergoing a continual process of decay. That process causes a decrease in the complexity of all things. Yet evolution requires the opposite to occur—namely, that all things evolve from a simple state to a state of greater complexity. For many years, evolutionists have tried to reconcile the paradox that exists between evolution and the Second Law of Thermodynamics. In contrast to evolution, the position of creationists is consistent with the all-important Second Law of Thermodynamics.

M any, if not most, educated people throughout the world believe that life originated from non-life (abiogenesis) by natural processes. Following the laws of physics and chemistry, the concept is that through 'natural selection' operating over vast periods of time, fortuitous favourable events happened that brought about successively more complex biological chemicals, which again, either fortuitously or through some undefined inherent property of matter, concatenated, leading upward to protocells, cells, living creatures and then man himself. 'Natural selection' processes are such that biologic or pre-biologic products occurring in any given environmental niche that favour that niche are the ones that propagate and reproduce, and that random changes in either or both the environment and the progeny that are more appropriate for the new conditions will be the ones favoured to expand into the future. In a single paragraph, this is the general theory of Neo-Darwinian evolution.

The above stands in stark contrast to creationism, which holds that

Excerpted from *In Six Days: Why 50 Scientists Choose to Believe in Creation*, by Ker C. Thomson. Reprinted with permission from New Leaf Press, Inc.

currently observable natural processes are quite inadequate to explain the origin of life or its current, enormous observable complexity and variability. Rather, it postulates that a great creative mind must lie behind the origin of our observable universe and its living creatures—a mind and power vastly greater than anything of which man is capable. The questions of how long the creative process was and when it occurred vary from one creationist to another, but the concept of an original conscious creative act by a Creator who is distinct from His creation is common to all creationist viewpoints considered here.

Both creationists and evolutionists, by and large, concur that the evolutionary scenario outlined in the first paragraph above is highly improbable. It gains whatever credibility it enjoys only through the apparent availability of enormous amounts of time during which the most improbable events might conceivably occur.

It should be apparent that evolution is capable of an immediate scientific test: Is there available a scientifically observable process in nature which on a long-term basis is tending to carry its products upward to higher and higher levels of complexity? Evolution absolutely requires this.

Evolution and the Second Law

Evolution fails the test. The test procedure is contained within the Second Law of Thermodynamics. This law has turned out to be one of the surest and most fundamental principles in all of science. It is in fact used routinely in science to test postulated or existing concepts and machines (for instance perpetual motion machines, or a proposed chemical reaction) for viability. Any process, procedure or machine which would violate this principle is discarded as impossible. The Second Law of Thermodynamics states that there is a long-range decay process which ultimately and surely grips everything in the universe that we know about. That process produces a break-down of complexity, not its increase. This is the exact opposite of what evolution requires.

The argument against evolution presented above is so devastating in its scientific impact that, on scientific grounds, evolution would normally be immediately rejected by the scientific community. Unfortunately, for the preservation of truth, evolution is not adhered to on scientific grounds at all. Rather, it is clung to, though flying in the face of reason, with an incredible, fanatical, and irrational religious fervour. It loudly claims scientific support when, in fact, it has none worthy of the name.

If the evolution or creationism discussion were decided by sensible appeals to reason, evolution would long ago have joined the great philosophical foolishnesses of the past, with issues such as how many angels can dance on the head of a pin, or the flat-earth concept.

To bury evolutionary faith, then, it seems necessary to look beyond the general Second Law argument presented above to the specific details, and to consider and dispose of the quibbles raised by the evolutionary community.

One objection that can be posited to the preceding argument is that the Second Law deals with long-term results, or equilibrium states, in more chemical language. An evolutionary response then is that evolution must be somehow tucked in between the successive equilibrium states.

Reconsider the implications of the evolutionary theory's requirements for large time spans. Is it not obvious that the Second Law of Thermodynamics is what is most pertinent here? The huge amounts of time available that evolution claims for itself will provide plenty of time for successive equilibrium states to be achieved and the Second Law of Thermodynamics to apply. The fast-moving intermediate states are irrelevant in the long range of time. The long-range end results of each chemical reaction will be what dominates the long ages of evolution. The clear and inescapable statement by the Second Law will be that the end results must be in a downward direction, not the upward direction evolution requires.

The Second Law of Thermodynamics states that there is a long-range decay process which ultimately and surely grips everything in the universe that we know about. . . . This is the exact opposite of what evolution requires.

A second quibble to consider is that of 'micro vs macro': could it be if we consider evolution from an atomic or molecular level (micro), rather than from the level of matter at the state where we can feel, see and touch it (macro), that evolution might be found tucked away among the infinitesimally small (i.e. among the molecules, atoms or subatomic particles)? This really won't do, however.

As a minor first consideration here, note that we do not feel or see atoms and molecules with our unaided senses or rarely even perceive them at all at the individual atomic-level by any process.

Importance of the Second Law

In other words, our knowledge and perceptions at the micro level are obtained through a maze of complex machines which are themselves constructed from a large assortment of assumptions and abstruse theories. (No denial of atomic theory is being made here. Rather, it is simply being put in relative perspective.) On the other hand, the laws of thermodynamics rest on direct observations of matter in the aggregate and require only relatively sure and simple observations for their truth to be evident. In terms of reliability it should be apparent that, in general, results deduced from the Second Law should weigh in a little higher on the truth scale than results deduced only from atomic or molecular considerations. (Note, however, that the Second Law is not confined solely to aggregate matter, but applies at the micro level also.)

Regardless of the considerations in the preceding paragraph, when the actual chemical reactions of life are considered, especially those that might be involved at its inception, we find that the reactions are balky and require high concentrations of the reactants in order to proceed at all. Obviously then, this consideration results in levying a requirement for aggregate amounts of matter. This places us precisely back in situations uncontestably dominated by the Second Law. Again the Second Law points to lower levels of complexity, not higher.

Another quibble about application of the Second Law is contained in the claim that the Second Law of Thermodynamics applies only in closed systems. This is nonsense of a high order. Surely all of us are familiar with the everyday expression of this law in open systems. (The humorous popular version of the Second Law is 'Murphy's Law: Whatever can go wrong will go wrong'.) Metals corrode, machines break down, our bodies deteriorate and we die. Constant maintenance and planning against contingencies are required if life is to be sustained for even a transitory period, such as the lifetime of the individual. Ultimately, the Second Law takes over, and our bodies return to dust and our automobiles to the junk yard. By the application of our minds, we can resist the demands of the Second Law temporarily. General evolution collapses around this concept, however, because at the initiation of the evolutionary process in antiquity, there was no mind available to construct purposive 'machines' to temporarily obviate the Second Law's demands. The idea that the Second Law can be confined to closed systems is a piece of confusion on the part of the proponent of such a concept.

If the evolution or creationism discussion were decided by sensible appeals to reason, evolution would long ago have joined the great philosophical foolishnesses of the past.

As an aside, note also an important implication for evolution implied in the last paragraph. The Second Law tells us clearly that life could never get started by the activities of matter and energy unaided by outside intelligence. If life could never get started, surely we have an incredible waste of intellectual talent going on around us as many minds try to follow the pathways of evolution upwards from something that never started in the first place!

Now let us come back to the question of closed systems. Consider an experiment to see if the Second Law is true. It will be necessary to create a closed system to do so, a system protected from any outside confusing inputs. In this way it will be possible to see what is happening in the system, independent of outside events. When this is done, it is indeed found that inside the system, the trend is downward to disorganisation, as the Second Law requires. What happens then in an open system is that at any point we see the sum of all the different downward trends acting there.

To believe that the Second Law applies only in closed systems is to confuse the experimental necessity for a closed system to test for the existence of the Second Law, with the actual actions of the Second Law evident in the open systems in which we live.

Laws of probability

There is another quibble levied against the anti-evolutionary arguments developed here. It has to do with the word 'randomness'. Refer to the very first paragraph defining evolution. Some evolutionists will quarrel with words like 'randomness' or 'fortuitous', but others will agree with this definition.

There are, then, two schools of evolutionary thought. Consider first the group who believe that evolution is due to the random concatenation of available materials and the laws of physics and chemistry.

This concept can be readily treated by the mathematical laws of probability. Several writers have done this. Probably the best known is Fred Hoyle. The procedure is to estimate probabilities at each individual step of a postulated evolutionary path and concatenate these to arrive at the probability of finding an evolutionary product at any point along that path. Before proceeding very far along the path, probabilities drop to values so low that the proper word to describe such happenings is impossible. Hoyle put it roughly like this: The probability that life arose by random processes is equivalent to believing that a tornado striking a junk yard would reassemble the trash and leave a completed, assembled and functioning Boeing 707 there.

The Second Law tells us clearly that life could never get started by the activities of matter and energy unaided by outside intelligence.

Then there is the evolutionary group who think that randomness is only a minor or non-existent aspect of evolution. Their perspective is that evolution is the inevitable outcome of the laws of physics and chemistry. This idea is even easier to test than the randomness concept. We simply note that one of the surest generalisations in all of physics and chemistry is the Second Law of Thermodynamics which, as we have already shown, completely devastates any idea that matter unaided by mind or outside involvement will proceed to higher levels of organisation.

Now we come to the evolutionists' quibble that the Second Law was different in the past from now. This is simply an adult wish fulfilment on the part of the evolutionist espousing such notions. Unless he assumes what he is trying to prove, he is left at this point with no reliable evidence whatever to support his thesis. Science relies on measurements. Measurements we make now oppose evolution totally. To point for support to conditions in the distant past, where they can't be measured, puts the evolutionists in the same intellectual camp as those who believe in the tooth fairy.

Circular reasoning

Despite the arguments against evolution presented above and particularly in the last paragraph, the evolutionist clinging to his faith may say 'Well, we are here, aren't we?' One may point out to him that he has just finished engaging in circular reasoning. That is, he has obviously attempted to support evolution by assuming that evolution is true and is what has led to his human existence and presence here.

When the circularity of his reasoning is pointed out to him, the evolutionist may then grope for evidence in the fossil record. But again he is trotting out another batch of circular reasoning. This is so because evolution is used to interpret the fossil record, so it cannot be used to justify evolution. To do so puts the proponent in the intellectual booby hatch. Whatever the explanation for the fossil record may be, it cannot be one that in effect denies the Second Law of Thermodynamics.

In fact, the most obvious feature of the fossil record is not upward synthesis but rather death and decay. We find strong evidence for the steady loss of species within the fossil record. This is more in consonance with the Second Law of Thermodynamics than with the upward growth posited by evolution.

Not all creationists hold to six-day creationism. This writer is of the opinion that the scriptural evidence somewhat favours the six-day position. The scientific evidence for a long age rests primarily on the selection of evidence favourable to the long-age position rather than to the evaluation of all available evidence.

6

The Second Law of Thermodynamics May Favor Evolution

Robert T. Pennock

Robert T. Pennock is assistant professor of philosophy at the University of Texas at Austin.

Creationists long have argued that evolution violates the universal second law of thermodynamics. The second law states that closed systems tend to become highly disordered over time. Since evolution involves an increase over time in the order of systems as they move from simple to complex, evolution would appear to be inconsistent with the second law of thermodynamics. Recent studies, however, have shown that this is not true. In fact, it is possible that the Second Law actually may play a creative role in evolution.

One of the most common arguments that creationists make against evolution is that it supposedly violates the second law of thermodynamics, which states that closed systems tend towards increased entropy over time. (Entropy is a measure of the energy in the system that is available to do work. "High" entropy refers to "low" energy states, that is, those that are more disordered and thus less capable of doing work.) How can it be that evolution can go against the inexorable trend toward greater entropy identified by the second law? This purportedly unanswerable question has in fact already been answered by scientists, many times; I will be brief since most of the new creationists, to their credit, seem to have recognized that the argument is fallacious and have stopped using it. We now usually hear it only from traditional Young Earth Creationists (YECs). At ICR's museum one finds a section devoted to the second law with a prominent plaque which praises it as the most basic universal scientific law, one which is accepted by scientists in all fields, and yet one that directly contradicts evolution. Why is it alleged to contradict evolution? Supposedly because evolution always involves an increase in the ordered complexity of systems, whereas the second law says systems must

46

invariably run towards disorder. This might sound rather devastating to someone unfamiliar with evolution and thermodynamics, but there are several significant misunderstandings in creationists' arguments regarding evolution and the second law which render their point specious.

Major misunderstandings

The first is a misunderstanding of evolution: evolution is *not* always toward increasing complexity. Species can and do become less complex in certain environments. For instance, parasitic species that were once free-living lost complexity as they evolved to become dependent upon their hosts. This might be considered an understandable confusion, since increasing complexity is certainly the more striking feature of evolution, but the mistake is symptomatic of the generally uninformed character of most creationist criticisms.

As we have seen, even as an approximation the second law is not violated by evolution. Indeed, the second law could turn out to be a driving force in the emergence and evolution of life.

The second misunderstanding is more significant. When presenting their argument from the second law, many creationists conveniently leave out the part of the definition that limits it to *closed* systems. A system is thermodynamically closed if no energy crosses its boundary, and it is open otherwise. Think of a closed system as a perfectly insulated box that no heat can flow into or out of. Objects within the box might be of different temperatures, and if so they will exchange energy (hotter objects cooling down, cooler objects warming up) until eventually all reach an equilibrium. That is the point at which no further work can be done, because work requires energy differences so that the energy can flow. (You can think of this on the model of a waterwheel set up on a dammed stream; for it to turn, the water must be able to flow from a higher to a lower point—a miller will get no work from a waterwheel set up in a lake.) In an open system, on the other hand, the box is not perfectly insulated, thus allowing the objects within to increase in free energy (decrease in entropy) if energy is flowing into it from outside. If the system of the waterwheel on the stream were closed, then the wheel would eventually stop, after all the water above the dam had flowed by and dissipated its energy. But it is not a closed system. Energy from the sun is constantly pouring in, evaporating the water so that it rises (i.e., so that it goes, thermodynamically and literally, uphill), falls as rain above the dam and keeps the stream flowing and thereby the waterwheel turning. The creationist argument fails to recognize that the second law applies only to closed systems and that the earth is an *open* system. Their misunderstanding goes deeper still, for even if the earth *were* a closed system, evolution would still be possible since, as we noted, some objects in the insulated box may (at least temporarily) decrease in entropy though the system *as a whole* moves towards equilibrium. Thus in neither case is there a contradiction between evolution and the second law.

Creationists have by now heard this explanation many times, so what is their response? The plaque on the wall at the ICR's museum simply adds the claim that increase in entropy applies not only in closed systems but in open systems too. What is one to make of such an argument? Since the second law explicitly applies only to closed systems, it is either a misunderstanding of the second law or else creationists have discovered a remarkable third thermodynamic law. A second response, made by ICR's full-time debater Duane Gish, is that being an open system is not sufficient for evolution and that energy conversion mechanisms are also required but that these do not exist. But no evolutionary theorist ever said that being an open system is *sufficient* for evolution (what is the Darwinian mechanism for, after all); they were simply showing that evolution does not violate the second law, in answer to the creationist challenge that it did. Gish's argument is particularly interesting since it indirectly admits the evolutionists' point but tries to hide this admission by shifting to a new challenge about the need for (purportedly nonexistent) energy conversion mechanisms. But he is wrong on this last point too, for there are plenty of energy conversion mechanisms. The energy stores of organisms do not simply run down until they are depleted, but rather, like the sun-driven rain refills the stream, are regularly replenished. Plants convert solar energy by photosynthesis and animals gain energy by eating plants and each other. These processes might not be optimally efficient but there is more than enough incoming energy to allow considerable waste. Globally, entropy has increased as the second law requires, but locally it has decreased. As the physicist Erwin Schrödinger put it in his classic work *What is Life?* living organisms can "remain aloof" from the second law "by continually drawing from [their] environment negative entropy . . . . What an organism feeds on is negative entropy."[1]

No closed systems

In reality there are no perfectly closed systems (except the universe as a whole), so for us to apply the second law in practice we can only do so as an *approximation* in those smaller systems in which energy exchange with the external environment is negligible. But, as we have seen, even as an approximation the second law is not violated by evolution. Indeed, the second law could turn out to be a driving force in the emergence and evolution of life. Physicist Ilya Prigogine won a Nobel Prize for his work showing how thermodynamical systems far from equilibrium can give rise to order, or what he called "dissipative structures," and this discovery has sparked an active research program into self-organization. Jeffrey Wicken, for example, argues that the second law might be involved in the production of order and information and that it could extend the Darwinian program by "establishing continuities between biotic and prebiotic evolution and in allowing organisms to be understood as elements in ecological patterns of energy flow with *macroscopic trends* operating over and above microscopic particulars."[2] Wicken's own particular view might or might not pan out, but he is just one of a variety of researchers who think that thermodynamic principles might underlie features of the evolutionary processes. In an introduction to a collection of articles from researchers dealing with this topic, philosopher of biology David Hull suggests that a theoretical reformulation might be under way and that "[o]ne of the ambiguities that might well disappear as both evolutionary theory and thermodynamics are reformulated is the sharp distinction between statistical disorder and organizational complexity. One theory might well emerge capable of handling both."[3] Stuart Kauffman has pursued this research program perhaps further than anyone, especially in his *The Origins of Order* (1989) and he argues that "[all] free-living systems are dissipative structures."[4] Such investigations are still in their very early stages, so it is too soon to say what light they will shed, but if these possibilities are borne out and entropy turns out to have a positive causal role in the emergence of life it will be a significant addition to the Darwinian mechanisms. Creationists are certainly wrong to say that evolution violates the second law and it would be particularly ironic if the law turns out to actually play a creative role in evolution.

Notes

1. Erwin Schrödinger, 1967 (1944). *What Is Life?* Cambridge: Cambridge University Press.

2. Jeffrey S. Wicken, 1987. *Evolution, Thermodynamics, and Information: Extending the Darwinian Program.* New York: Oxford University Press, p. 5.

3. Bruce H. Weber, David J. Depew, and James D. Smith, 1988. *Entropy, Information, and Evolution" New Perspectives on Physical and Biological Evolution.* Cambridge, MA: The MIT Press, p. 8.

4. Stuart Kauffman, 1995. *At Home in the Universe: The Search for the Laws of Self-Organization and Complexity.* New York: Oxford University Press, p. 21.

7

Life Originated by Design

Dean L. Overman

Dean L. Overman is a lawyer who has taught at the University of Virginia. The author of several books, he was appointed as a visiting scholar at Harvard for the purpose of writing his latest book, A Case Against Accident and Self-Organization.

The answers to three significant questions impact upon the issue of the origin of life. The questions are: Does mathematical possibility favor the chance formation of life? If mathematically impossible, were there other possible causes? Could chance have caused the formation of a universe in which life could exist? Since the answer to each of these questions is no, we should look beyond the physical sciences for information about the origin of life.

Many people today believe that life on Earth originated as a result of random accidents. Most of us vaguely recall having heard of scientific experiments involving mixtures of inanimate materials that are said to be similar to the "prebiotic soup" that existed before life began. The mixtures are hit with an electrical spark that simulates a lightning strike, and amino acids—building blocks of life—result. So we're assured that a similar accidental transformation long ago caused life to originate from non-living matter.

But in fact, recent discoveries in molecular biology, particle astrophysics, and the geological records raise profound doubts about all this. Three questions should be investigated: (1) Is it mathematically possible that accidental processes caused the first form of living matter? (2) If accident is mathematically impossible as the cause of the first form of living matter, are other popular scenarios that matter "self-organized" into life plausible? (3) Is it mathematically possible that accidental processes caused the formation of a universe that is compatible with life? In examining these questions, I will use the widely accepted scientific definition of life, which holds that living matter processes energy, stores information, and replicates.

To answer the first question—the likelihood that random accidents turned inanimate matter into living matter—I will address only the molecular biological aspects. Consider a calculation by the famous (atheist) scientist Sir Fred Hoyle. Hoyle understood that even the simplest living cells are extremely complex, containing many nucleic acids, enzymes, and molecules all joined together in a very precise sequence. He calculated the odds of each of 20 amino acids appearing in the correct sequence to form an enzyme as 1 chance in 10^{20}. Since the simplest living cell requires 2,000 functioning enzymes, the odds against the amino acids appearing in the correct sequence for a living cell were equal to 1 in $10^{20} \times 2,000$—or 1 chance in $10^{40,000}$. This number is a *1* followed by 40,000 zeros. Because mathematicians normally regard a chance of 1 in 10^{50} as mathematical impossibility, Hoyle concluded that life could not have appeared by earth-bound random processes, even if the whole universe consisted of prebiotic soup. His collaborator Chandra Wickramasinghe put it more dramatically: "The chances that life just occurred are about as unlikely as a typhoon blowing through a junkyard and constructing a Boeing 747."

Beyond mathematical possibility

To appreciate the size of 10^{50}, consider that if you assume the Big Bang occurred 15 billion years ago, only 10^{18} seconds have occurred in all of time. The number of atoms in the known universe is estimated to be only 10^{80}. Physicist Paul Davies has equated the odds of one chance in 10^{60} as equal to the odds against hitting a one-inch target with the random, unaimed shot of a rifle bullet from a distance of 20 billion light years. One chance in $10^{40,000}$ is far beyond mathematical possibility.

Actually the odds of life forming by random processes are even worse, for several reasons. First, scientists are discovering many reasons to think that conditions on Earth were not as the prebiotic soup experiments assume. Second, there is absolutely no physical evidence for the existence of either the prebiotic soup or many of the substances the experiments produced. In fact, evidence of prebiotic soup that should have been left behind in geological records does *not* exist. Third, even if amino acids did form in an ancient prebiotic soup, there are still astronomical odds against those amino acids joining together to form even very short proteins, much less the DNA found in all life.

Worst of all, recent discoveries in the fossil records reveal that only 130 million years were actually available for life to appear on Earth by accidental processes. The Earth formed about 4.6 billion years ago, but was too torrid to support life until about 3.98 billion years ago. Fossil records discovered recently (particularly in the Istaq complex in Greenland) show life existed at least 3.85 billion years ago. That means only 130 million years were available for random processes to form the first living matter, not the billions of years we once thought. This makes the odds even more remote that accidental processes would have produced the first form of living matter. Chance had no chance to form life.

Our second question concerned the plausibility of current theories that matter "self-organized" itself into life according to the laws of physics and chemistry. To understand the idea of self-organization, we must recall the Second Law of Thermodynamics, which requires that any system near equilibrium will always move toward disorder (also known as entropy). Yet sometimes an energy flow can cause disordered inanimate matter to organize spontaneously into an ordered system. Consider this example: Picture a bathtub filled with water where the water molecules are in equilibrium—warmer water is mixed evenly with cooler water so that the water molecules are all at an even temperature and distributed in a totally random, unordered manner. Pulling the drain plug allows the force of gravity to move the water from this chaotic, random state of equilibrium into an ordered vortex. This example demonstrates how an energy flow (such as that derived from the force of gravity) can move a system away from equilibrium and cause the spontaneous creation of order.

Could a similar sort of self-organization create life? Well, living matter must contain sufficient complex information (or instructions) to be able to maintain and replicate itself. Here information theory is useful, because it allows us to quantify the amount of information in living and non-living matter in terms of bits and bytes.

The enormous information in living matter involves irregular, flexible patterns, while inanimate matter never rises above simple, repeating patterns in its information content. A quartz crystal, for example, has simple order and replicates, but it has very little information content and is not alive. By contrast, DNA exists in all living matter and contains a vast amount of information that allows organisms to replicate and maintain themselves, that is, to live. The DNA for even the smallest single-celled bacterium contains over 4 million instructions. These instructions are encoded in DNA's four "bases"—the rungs of the famous double helix ladder of DNA that are denoted A, G, C, T. The bases act like a four-letter alphabet for the genetic process. This process, like the English language, consists of a code. Acting like sentences, DNA instructions pass on the information needed to form a protein or some other necessity that the living organism needs in order to replicate or maintain itself.

The problem with self-organization theorists is that the mechanisms they claim could create life lack any plausible method of generating the sort of information DNA contains. Their scenarios only describe the formation of *order*, not complex *information*. They like to use the term "complexity" in their work, but all they mean by it is highly organized, intricate patterns, which is not a definition capable of distinguishing quartz crystals from rhododendrons or amoebae.

Chance had no chance to form life.

Self-organization scenarios claim that the laws of physics (and the laws of chemistry they produce) caused the formation of living matter. But this idea faces a grave obstacle—the simple mathematical fact that the genetic information contained in even the smallest living organism is much larger than the information content found in the laws of physics, as Hubert Yockey, a Manhattan Project physicist, noted in *Information Theory and Molecular Biology*. Where did the greater information content of life come from? This fundamental difficulty has not been addressed by the theorists of self-organization.

Even if we ignore this fundamental mathematical fact, there is also the problem that the laws of physics only produce regular patterns. DNA—life—requires an irregular pattern to transmit information through the genetic code. To use an analogy to the code in our written English language, if I type the letters "ABC" repeatedly for 1,000 pages, I would have a highly ordered, regular, predictable pattern such as a law of nature would produce. But I would have conveyed very little information. The *Oxford History of the American People*, on the other hand, has an irregular pattern in its alphabet letters, and it conveys a large amount of information. Similarly, DNA varies its letters A, C, T, G in order to transmit the genetic code.

Flexibility and the lack of a regular, predictable pattern in DNA argue against the existence of an inherent law that controls the operation of DNA. A physical law produces a regular, predictable pattern, such as the law of gravity produced in the ordered vortex of water in our bathtub example. If DNA were caused by such a law, it would have a simple repeating sequence (like ABCABC) without much information. And DNA would not be capable of transmitting millions of instructions, as it does in even the simplest living organism.

The Oxford chemist Michael Polanyi recognized this in 1953. Just as the information contained in a poem is not determined by the chemicals in the pen used to write the poem, so the information in the genetic code, although encoded in a four-letter alphabet, is not determined by the chemical elements of that alphabet.

One can only speculate whether an adequate self-organization theory will ever be discovered. At present we must conclude that the information content required in the simplest living form of matter could not have arisen only from the laws of physics and chemistry.

Let us turn to our third question, which involves particle astrophysics and the likelihood of a universe forming in such a way as to be compatible with life. Many proponents of chance as the cause of life proposed their theories when the universe was believed to be in a steady state and infinitely old. In an infinite, ageless universe, anything can happen, but now scientists view the universe as young, expanding from a definite beginning, and approximately 15 billion years old.

Contemporary physics has also discovered that the physical universe appears to be precisely fine tuned in numerous ways that accommodate the formation of life. At the very outset of the Big Bang, the mass of the elementary particles, the strength of the four forces, and the values of the fundamental constants were very precise. Imagine that you are selecting the values for these natural quantities by twiddling a vast number of knobs. You would find that almost all knob settings would render the universe uninhabitable. All these many knobs would have to be fine tuned to enormous precision if life is to flourish in the universe.

A fine tuned universe

In fact, our universe is so remarkably fine tuned to allow for the origination of life that one may think of it as a finely sharpened pencil standing vertically on its graphite point in a precarious balance. Any deviation in a myriad of physical values would cause the pencil to tilt, fall, and preclude the formation of life. The fine tuning is exactly what is required not just for one reason, but for two or three or five reasons. Accidental processes could not plausibly tune these fundamental astrophysical values first one way and then another to satisfy conflicting requirements for the development of life.

There are many examples of this extraordinary fine tuning, but consider only a few:

• *Fine tuning in the formation of carbon.* Life would be impossible without carbon, and yet because of the precise requirements for its existence, the carbon atom should be very scarce. The formation of a carbon atom requires a rare triple collision known as the triple alpha process. The first step in this process occurs when a helium nucleus collides with another helium nucleus within a star. This collision produces an unstable, very ephemeral isotope of beryllium. When the unstable, short-lived beryllium collides with a third helium nucleus, a carbon nucleus is formed. Astrophysicist Sir Fred Hoyle predicted the resonances (or energy levels) of the carbon and oxygen atoms. The resonance of the carbon nucleus is precisely the right resonance to enable the components to hold together rather than disperse. This resonance perfectly matches the combined resonance of the third helium nucleus and the beryllium atom. Hoyle admitted that his atheism was dramatically disturbed when he calculated the odds against the precise matching required to form a carbon atom through this triple alpha process. He said the number he calculated from the facts is so overwhelming as to put almost beyond question the conclusion that a superintellect had monkeyed with the laws of physics.

Accidental processes could not plausibly tune these fundamental astrophysical values first one way and then another to satisfy conflicting requirements for the development of life.

• *Explosive power of Big Bang precisely matched to the force of gravity.* Physicist Paul Davies calculated that the matching of the explosive force of the Big Bang and gravity had to match to one part in 10^{60}. If the explosive force were only slightly higher, the universe would consist of gas without stars or planets. If the force were reduced by one part in a thousand billion, the universe would have collapsed back to a singular point after a few million years.

• *Fine tuning in the strong and weak nuclear force.* The strong force which binds the particles in an atom's nucleus must be balanced with the weak nuclear force to a degree of one part in 10^{60}. If the strong force were any weaker, atomic nuclei could not hold together and only hydrogen would exist. If the strong force were only slightly stronger, hydrogen would be an unusual element, the Sun would not exist, water would not exist, and the heavier elements necessary for life would not be available.

• *Fine tuning of electromagnetic force and ratio of electron mass to proton mass and proton mass to neutron mass.* Any deviation in the strength of the electromagnetic force would also preclude the molecular formation necessary for life. The electromagnetic force must be precisely balanced with the ratio of electron mass to proton mass. The proton is 1,836 times heavier than the electron. This fundamental ratio must be very finely adjusted to make life possible. Moreover, the mass of the proton and the mass of the neutron are meticulously balanced. The emergence of life depended on an astounding precision among the masses of these three particles.

• *Fine tuning of the order at the initial Big Bang.* The Second Law of Thermodynamics requires that disorder in the universe tends toward a maximum. Because the universe could not have been dissipating from infinity or it would have run down, it must have had a beginning—a very highly ordered beginning. If the Big Bang is regarded as only an impressive accident, there is no explanation why it produced a universe with such a high degree of order, contrary to the Second Law.

Physical laws cannot explain life's origins

Oxford mathematician Roger Penrose calculated that at the very beginning of the Big Bang, the precision required to set the universe on its highly ordered course in which life could develop was staggering: "an accuracy of one part in $10^{10^{123}}$." Penrose adds, "This is an extraordinary figure. One could not possibly even write the number down in full, in the ordinary denary notation; it would be *1* followed by 10^{123} successive *0s*! Even if we were to write a *0* on each separate proton and on each separate neutron in the entire universe—and we could throw in all the other particles as well for good measure—we should fall far short of writing down the figure needed."

• *Fine tuning in the precision between counter-intuitive abstract mathematics and the physical world.* An accidental universe cannot explain the astounding agreement between abstract mathematics and the laws of the physical world. Abstract mathematics have predicted counter-intuitive phenomena to a remarkable precision. For example, the agreement between the counter-intuitive theory of general relativity and the physical world has been confirmed by experience to more than one-trillionth of a percent. Precision to this degree cannot be explained by chance alone. Similarly, the strange, unseen, counter-intuitive subatomic world of quantum mechanics matches the predictions of abstract mathematics to a remarkable degree. Our minds seem to be finely tuned to the structure of the universe. This fine tuning cannot be understood as a curious spin-off from the need of our ancestors to dodge a wild animal.

An accidental universe cannot explain the astounding agreement between abstract mathematics and the laws of the physical world.

Because the mathematical probabilities against life arising by accident are so overwhelming in our universe, some scientists are attracted to the concept of an "oscillating" universe in which, crudely put, there is an infinite cycle of Big Bangs and Big Crunches as the universe expands and contracts. This would permit an infinite number of beginnings. Since infinity can be used to explain almost anything, a person displeased with the unlikeliness of an accident causing life to form may grasp at any opportunity to bring infinity into the picture. Stephen Hawking and Roger Penrose, however, have demonstrated that the gravitational force in a collapsing universe would produce a Big Crunch that would be totally chaotic, and the entropy at the Crunch would be so large that it would preclude another expansion.

There are other abstruse theories that try to concoct similar scenarios in which the universe didn't begin in the Big Bang but somehow always existed. Those who put such theories forward implicitly recognize that if the universe did have a beginning and did arise out of nothing, then something must have caused it. I deal with these theories in my book *A Case Against Accident and Self-Organization*, where I show that they suffer from the same sort of physical and logical difficulties as the oscillating universe theory.

In sum, the case against chance as the cause of life is satisfied completely by the probabilities involved in the fine tuning of particle astrophysics. When one couples these probabilities with the molecular biological probabilities we've considered, the compounded calculation wipes the idea of accident entirely out of court.

Nor does a plausible self-organization theory exist. The answer to the question of life's formation will not be found in the laws of physics and chemistry, because life transcends those laws in the vast information it possesses and in the irregular flexible patterns it uses to convey this information. The physical sciences, in short, lead us to conclude that life is more than a physical thing, which means we should be open-minded about the possibility that other fields of study can teach us something about the origin and meaning of life.

8

New Creationists and Their Discredited Arguments

Michael Ruse

Michael Ruse is professor of philosophy and zoology at Canada's University of Guelph. The author of Taking Darwin Seriously *and* But Is It Science?, *he participated in a debate on creationism and evolution on "Firing Line" in December 1997.*

A new school of creationism has arisen from the ashes of the old. Its proponents offer the same arguments as before with one major difference, namely, reliance upon science to support the biblical argument of a six-day creation and a six thousand-year-old earth. Despite the new creationists' claims to the contrary, their work has failed to disprove Darwinian evolution. Like their predecessors, they ignore empirical evidence that does not support their claims.

To the working scientist, and not just the biologist, it is simply ludicrous to think that there is any question about the natural origin of organisms from forms very different—ultimately, from inorganic materials. This is as much a fact of nature as that the earth goes around the sun or that water is made from oxygen and hydrogen. But it is certainly not a fact to many nonscientists, especially not to those influenced by North American evangelical Christianity. Again and again, one hears: "Evolution is a theory and not a fact," or some such thing. People tend not to unpack this wise-sounding statement, but of one thing you can be sure: "theory" is a euphemism for "false."

Recently, the naysayers have gained more authority as their ranks have been swelled by people of distinction and position—not biologists working on the problems that concern evolutionists, but from other areas of science as well as branches of the humanities including philosophy. I shall examine proposals that these critics have made as an alternative to evolution through selection, in particular, the pretensions of the supposedly new hypothesis about "irreducible complexity," a phenomenon that demands the invocation of a Supreme Being of some sort. This is a very old argument in-

Reprinted from "Answering the Creationists," by Michael Ruse, *Free Inquiry*, Spring 1998. Reprinted with permission.

deed. Far from being a genuine alternative to evolutionism, it is neither needed nor plausible. On its own terms, it is riddled with problems.

Darwin's critics

Creationism is the belief that the Bible is literally true. One must conclude that the earth and its denizens were created miraculously some 6,000 years ago, in six days of 24-hour duration, that humans appeared last, and that at some later point the earth was totally submerged by water. It is an American invention of the past century. Scorned by mainline churches as well as by scientists, it has nevertheless shown considerable staying power. In the 1960s, thanks to the efforts of a Bible scholar John C. Whitcomb and hydraulic engineer Henry M. Morris, authors of *Genesis Flood,* creationism took on a whole new life, leading eventually to court trials as certain states of the American South tried to insist that the children in their public schools be taught creationism as a viable alternative alongside evolution. Beaten back in this attempt, it seemed that perhaps creationism was at last defeated, but phoenix-like it has arisen again, and as the century comes to an end is perhaps showing more life—certainly more respectability—than at any time previously.

It seemed that perhaps creationism was at last defeated, but phoenix-like it has arisen again.

The new creationists are wary of indiscriminate labeling. Most of them do admit to religious beliefs, but they are much aware of the ridicule that has been heaped on those who deny physics to the extent of claiming the falsity of an earth of more than a few thousand years of age. I suspect that most of these people are not in fact "young earthers"; but whatever the minutiae of their beliefs, one finds that inasmuch as these new arrivals accept the name of "creationist," it is usually defined in such a broad way as to be compatible with a great deal of science, even a little bit of evolution if one is so inclined. These new arrivals, whether from conviction or expediency, have tended—at least, until recently—to stay very carefully away from explications of their own positions.

My main concern is with the case made by Berkeley Professor of Law Phillip Johnson, author of *Darwin on Trial* (1991). This has been an immensely popular book. The most striking thing about Johnson's work and the others following in its trail is that its attack is curiously shallow. One would never guess that there is at stake on the evolution side a whole discipline, with departments and students and journals and conferences and much much more. What one would infer rather is that there are three or four writers in the popular domain and these—principally Stephen Jay Gould with one or two uncertain allies like Richard Dawkins—are basically the beginning and end of evolutionary biology today. So straight off, the case is slanted against evolutionism: the level tends to that of pop science rather than professional science. One searches in vain in the writings of Johnson and his fellow new creationists for any of the exciting discoveries and theories of today that make evolution such a vibrant area of research: the findings of molecular evolutionists thanks to brilliant work on gel electrophoresis by Richard Lewontin, for instance, or the work of the sociobiologists following up the ideas of William Hamilton or John Maynard Smith. There is nothing on the ways in which, using modern thinking about natural selection, students of the social insects have been able to tease apart the relationships between workers and queens and drones. As Thomas Kuhn and other students of the theory of science have rightly stressed repeatedly, in judging a theory or paradigm or new area of science, one must ask as much about the new directions it uncovers as about problems one might have with foundations.

What of the science that is actually discussed? There is a constant confusing of the *fact* of evolution, and with the *path* or paths of evolution, and then with the *cause* or mechanisms of evolution. Making Gould today's leading evolutionist makes the job much easier than it might otherwise be. His theory of punctuated equilibria is paraded out; its postulation of rapid change between periods of nonactivity is taken as evidence of evolutionists' problems with the paths of evolution; and then all is wrapped up as a supposedly devastating critique of the very fact of evolution.

We must not be bullied by the creationists' strategy. They may ignore it but let us continue to be guided by the threefold division of fact, path, and cause. What has Johnson (and his fellows) to say about the fact of evolution? The key to understanding the evolutionist's conviction of the fact of evolution lies in the total evidence-appealing consilience at its heart—the very same kind of consilience that is at the heart of legal practice, as prosecutors try to pin guilt on defendants through circumstantial evidence. There is nothing on this method of argumentation: a curious omission, especially given that Johnson is an academic lawyer specializing in criminal law. One consequence of this omission is that Johnson and others can avoid talking about all of the evidence, quite ignoring such crucial planks in the evolutionist's case as biogeography.

The Cambrian explosion

Move next to questions of path, an area that has always been a happy hunting ground for creationists—failure to find early life forms, the Cambrian explosion, the gaps in the fossil record thereafter, and so forth. To quote another of the new creationists:

> Before the Cambrian era, a brief 600 million years ago, very little is inscribed in the fossil record; but then, signaled by what I imagine is a spectral puff of smoke and a deafening ta-da!, an astonishing number of novel biological structures come into creation, and they come into creation at once.

> Thereafter, the major transitional sequences are incomplete.[1]

What can one say in response, except: "Go and look at the evidence, go and look at the explanations that evolutionists are offering, and then if you still disagree, let us discuss and argue. But not before. Until you do this, you have not the authority to make such claims as this." Take that truly remarkable explosion of life half a billion years ago, in the Cambrian. Leading American paleontologist John Sepkoski has put forward a theory showing how this increase is a direct function of population growth—it is precisely the exponential rise one expects when a group is colonizing a new ecological space. He argues also that this explains why the rise comes to an end, why the early forms then declined in numbers, why we later get another rise, and much more. He may be right. He may be wrong. But he is worthy of attention. Which he does not get. Tripping through Gould and Dawkins is no substitute for real work.

Take a favorite argument of the creationists: there is a lack of transitional fossils between the land animals and the marine animals, like whales. Now these gaps are being filled.

Most remarkable of all is Johnson's treatment of that old chestnut, the gaps in the record. Expectedly, archaeopteryx—the reptile-bird—gets short shrift. None of the intermediate features gets an airing.

It is of course just not true that archaeopteryx is the only bridging fossil known to evolutionists. Take a favorite argument of the creationists: there is a lack of transitional fossils between the land animals and the marine animals, like whales. Now these gaps are being filled. Proto-whales have been discovered. We really do have fossil marine mammals with rudimentary limbs, on the way to the organisms of today but not yet there. Do not, however, expect an apology and a retraction.

> Even the vestigial limbs [of supposed whale ancestors] present problems. By what Darwinian process did useful hind limbs wither away to vestigial proportions, and at what stage in the transformation from rodent to sea monster did this occur? Did rodent forelimbs transform themselves by gradual adaptive stages into whale flippers? We hear nothing of the difficulties because to Darwinists unsolvable problems are not important."[2]

In any case, can we be sure that these supposed limbs really were connected with the proto-whales? Perhaps they were just lying nearby.

I will treat this kind of argumentation with the silent contempt that it merits—although I would love to know where Johnson got the idea that whales are descended from rodents. (Truly, their ancestors were closest to the ancestors of the herbivores like cows. Rodents belong to another branch, along with rabbits.)

I will move on to the question of causes or mechanisms. Here we find the new creationists trembling with critical ecstasy. Once again natural selection is brought out, paraded, and found wanting. Either it is a tautology, necessarily true and thus immune to the evidence, or it is open to checking and has been found wanting. Supposedly, even evolutionists recognize this, as they rush to alternative mechanisms like Gouldian punctuated equilibria. Either way, selection doesn't amount to much. But indeed, apart from all of the problems with mutations, apart from the false analogy with artificial selection, apart from the fact that no one has ever seen it do more than the bare minimum, in the opinion of the critics, natural selection is conceptually flawed—through and through. It simply cannot produce the designlike features that characterize the world: the adaptations so necessary for life and limb.

As so often in discussions of this kind, we encounter the analogy of monkeys typing Shakespeare—or rather of monkeys not typing Shakespeare. Random hitting on a typewriter is not going to produce *Hamlet*, nor is natural selection working on random mutation going to produce organisms.

This is a false analogy. Natural selection is not like monkeys simply hitting the keys and, if wrong, starting again from the beginning. Selection is cumulative. Once one has made some progress, that stays on as backing for all subsequent tries. And selection does not demand one particular predetermined play, and that the best ever written. In evolution, there is no already-decided end point. Any play will do—an appalling farce, for instance—and all it has to be is better than any rival. To think otherwise is to show, truly, that you do not know what you are talking about. Worse, it is to show that you do not know what evolutionists are talking about.

Irreducible complexity

Perhaps encouraged by their self-awarded success, the new creationists have recently started to break from their strategy of unrelenting attack. Thanks to biochemist Michael J. Behe, author of *Darwin's Black Box: The Biochemical Challenge to Evolution* (1996), they have started to lift the veil from their own beliefs about origins *qua* science. Indeed, one might say they have ripped the veil in twain with trumpets accompanying: "The result is so unambiguous and so significant that it must be ranked as one of the greatest achievements in the history of science. The discovery rivals those of Newton and Einstein, Lavoisier and Schrodinger, Pasteur and Darwin."

It is Behe's claim that there are facts of organic nature whose origin cannot be evolutionary. Cannot in fact be natural at all, meaning the consequence of regular unguided law. These facts, marked by irreducible complexity, have to be the product of a designer, however construed.

> By *irreducibly complex* I mean a single system composed of several well-matched, interacting parts that contribute to the basic function, wherein the removal of any one of the parts causes the system to effectively cease functioning. An irreducibly complex system cannot be produced directly (that is, by continuously improving the initial function, which continues to work by the same mechanism) by slight, successive modifications of a precursor system, because any precursor to an irreducibly complex system that is missing a part is by definition nonfunctional. An irreducibly complex biological system, if there is such a thing, would be a powerful challenge to Darwinian evolution. Since natural selection can only choose systems that are already working, then if a biological system cannot be produced gradually it would have to arise as an integrated unit, in one fell swoop, for natural selection to having anything to act on.

Behe does not want to rule out a natural origin for all irreducible complexities, but we learn that, as the complexity rises, the likelihood of getting things by any indirect natural route "drops precipitously." As a physical example of an irreducibly complex system, Behe instances a mousetrap—something with five parts (base, spring, hammer, and so forth), any one of which is individually necessary for the mousetrap's functioning. It could not have come into being naturally in one step and it could not have come gradually—any piece would not function properly and any part missing would mean failure of the whole. It had to be designed and made by a conscious being: a fact that is true also of organisms. Behe instances the phenomenon of blood clotting as an organic example of such intelligent design. "The purposeful arrangement of parts" is the name of the game.

The new creationism is no more effective than any of the earlier versions.

As it happens, Behe's choice of a mousetrap as an exemplar of intelligent design has been somewhat unfortunate. All sorts of parts can be eliminated or twisted and adapted to other ends. There is no need to use a base, for example. You can just attach the units directly to the floor: a move that at once reduces the trap's components from five to four. But even if the mousetrap were a terrific example, it would hardly make Behe's point. No evolutionist ever claimed that all of the parts of a functioning organic feature had to be in place at once, nor did any evolutionist ever claim that a part used now for one end had always to have that function. Ends get changed, and something introduced for one purpose might well take on another purpose: only later might it get fixed in as essential.

Against the mousetrap, let me take the example of an arched bridge, with stones meeting in the middle and with no supporting cement. If you tried to build it from scratch, the two sides would keep collapsing as you started to move the higher stones into the middle. What you must do first is build an understructure, placing the stones on it: then, when the stones are pressing against one another in the middle, you can remove the understructure. It is now no longer needed; although, if you were not aware that it had once been there you might think that it is a miracle that the bridge ever was built. Likewise in evolution: some pathway (say) exists; a set of parts sit idle on the pathway; then these parts link up; and finally the old pathway is declared redundant and removed by selection. Only the new pathway exists, although without the old one the new one would have been impossible.

Behe is a real scientist, but his case for the impossibility of a small-step natural origin of biological complexity has been trampled upon contemptuously by the scientists working in the field. They think his grasp of the pertinent science is weak and his knowledge of the literature curiously (although conveniently) outdated.

For example, far from the evolution of clotting being a mystery, the past three decades of work by Russell Doolittle and others has thrown significant light on the ways in which clotting came into being. More than this, it can be shown that the clotting mechanism does not have to be a one-step phenomenon with everything already in place and functioning. One step in the cascade involves fibrinogen, required for clotting, and another, plaminogen, required for clearing clots away. Doolittle writes:

> It has become possible during the last decade to "knock out" genes in experimental organisms. "Knock out mice" are now a common (but expensive) tool in the armamentarium of those scientists anxious to cure the world's ills. Recently the gene for plaminogen was knocked out of mice and, predictably, those mice had thrombotic complications because fibrin clots could not be cleared away. Not long after that, the same workers knocked out the gene for fibrinogen in another line of mice. Again, predictably, those mice were ailing, although in this case hemorrhage was the problem. And what do you think happened when these two lines of mice were crossed? For all practical purposes the mice lacking both genes were normal. Contrary to claims about irreducible complexity, the entire ensemble of proteins is *not* needed. Music and harmony can arise from a smaller orchestra.[3]

Suppose you accept Behe's conclusion about the existence of a Designer. What precisely is the role of this Designer? Behe is careful not to identify it with the Christian God. But let us suppose such a Designer does exist and is at work producing irreducibly complex organisms. Who then is responsible when things go wrong? What about mal-mutations causing such awful things as Tay-Sachs disease and sickle-cell anemia? Behe says that raising this problem is raising the problem of evil, which is so. But labeling the problem does not make it go away.

Darwinism as religion

The new creationism is no more effective than any of the earlier versions. But I doubt that my counter-arguments will have much effect, and not simply because these critics are blind or biased. There is more at stake than has hitherto been acknowledged. The real problem with Darwinism for the new creationists lies not in its status as science. The real objection is to Darwinism as religion.

To the new creationists, Darwinism is a wolf in sheep's clothing. Secular religion in the clothing of empirical science. Darwinism is based on a philosophy—the philosophy of "naturalism." "Darwinian evolution is an imaginative story about who we are and where we came from, which is to say a creation myth. As such it is an obvious starting point for speculation about how we ought to live and what we ought to value."[4] From here it is but a short step to sex, drugs, and contempt for capitalism.

If there is a connection between fact and value, between Darwinism and people's systems of value, it is far from obvious that this has to be one of freedom and permissiveness, of sexual laxity, and of personal autonomy. There have been Darwinians of the political and moral and religious right of a kind to make Johnson and his fellows look like escapees from the 1960s. Sir Ronald Fisher, for example, is certainly the most distinguished theoretical biologist in the history of evolutionary thought. He was also a Christian, a member of the Church of England, a conservative, a member of the British Establishment, and one whose social views were somewhere to the right of Louis XIV.

Johnson draws a distinction between "methodological naturalism," the attitude by the scientist that one should explain as far as is possible in terms of natural unbroken laws, and "metaphysical naturalism," the belief that unbroken-law-governed material is all there is to existence. Unfortunately, argues Johnson, the scientist starts off down the path of methodological naturalism and ends up with metaphysical naturalism. And this spells atheism, which in turn leads to complete moral license.

To the new creationists, Darwinism is a wolf in sheep's clothing. Secular religion in the clothing of empirical science.

There are people who are fully committed to methodological naturalism, believing that evolution is true, and who yet are theists in as meaningful a sense as one could ever wish. The present pope—a man, incidentally, who is notoriously tough on such things as sexuality—is precisely such a person. Recently, Pope John Paul II has come out four-square in favor of evolution and yet he reserves to God His traditional full power of action.

Finishing the argument against Johnson, the evolutionist notes that his moral worries are no more well taken than his fears for theism. Even if Darwinism were to imply atheism, there is no logical reason to think that such a person would thereby be committed to moral nihilism. In the last century, although people like Thomas Henry Huxley described themselves as agnostics, they were certainly atheistic with respect to Johnson's kind of God. Yet they were moral—boringly and obsessively moral—in a very conventional manner. Huxley met and admired George Eliot; but, given that she lived openly with a man to whom she was not married, he would not invite her to his own house to meet his wife and children.

The new creationists are right in seeing evolutionary ideas as a threat, although they are hardly right in laying at the evolutionists' door all of the moral moves of modern society. I suspect that, like most of us, evolutionists reflect their place in this society as much as they create it.

The new creationism is a slicker product than the old creationism. Exploring the fears of its exponents leads us to think more carefully about Darwinism and its nature and limits. But, ultimately, there is nothing to challenge Darwin's work. It is time, as the title of my book suggests, for *Taking Darwin Seriously*.

Notes

1. D. Berlinski, "The deniable Darwin," *Commentary* June 1996: 19–29.

2. P.E. Johnson, *Darwin on Trial*, 1991. (Washington, D.C.: Regnery Gateway) p. 87.

3. Russell E. Doolittle, "A delicate balance," *Boston Review* 22 (1997): no. 1: 28–29.

4. *Darwin on Trial*, p. 133.

9

The Fossil Record Supports Evolution

David A. Thomas

David A. Thomas is a professional sculptor who has produced detailed scientific replicas of dinosaurs and other ancient life forms for museums all over the world. An avid fossil enthusiast, he described his study of a Paluxy River trackway showing a theropod attack on a sauropod dinosaur in a feature article in the December 1997 Scientific American.

The argument by creationists that gaps in the fossil record invalidate the concept of evolution has little merit. For one thing, fossils are not plentiful since fossilization is dependent upon a complicated series of steps occurring in sequence. However, the relative shortage of fossils should not invalidate the merit and value of those fossils that we do find. The Morrison Formation in the western United States is one example of a fossil preserve that offers a relatively full and coherent picture of prehistoric life.

C reationists often point out that the fossil record has gaps, and they seem to think that those parts we do have are somehow invalidated because we don't have the entire record. It's as if the books in the public library were somehow made worthless because the library doesn't have every book ever published. The creationists' dream world is a sort of paleontological Forest Lawn Cemetery where all animals (and people) are carefully laid out and preserved. That this idealized concept does not conform to the jumbled, chaotic, infinitely complicated real world is in no way a failure of the real world. It is a failure of the concept.

Formation of a fossil

Of course there are gaps in the fossil record, and always will be. For a fossil to be found, a complicated series of steps must occur in sequence. The first is that the animal (or plant) must be buried quickly. Animals that die on the plains or in the mountains are soon found by scavengers, such as hyenas or ceratosaurs, and soon reduced to bone chips. Most animals that

Reprinted from "Gaps in the Fossil Record: A Case Study," by David A. Thomas, *Skeptical Inquirer*, November/December 1998. Reprinted with permission.

are fossilized are caught in a flash flood, or die in or near a river and are buried in a sand bar or an overbank flood, or are caught in a sandstorm. If the current in the river is fairly strong, even those few animals that die in the water are soon torn apart and their bones scattered over acres of river bottom. It is estimated that perhaps one animal in a thousand is fossilized, likely a generous estimate.

Evolutionary changes tend to occur in small, isolated communities, and the new animals then move into the general territory and supplant their relatives there.

The second condition necessary for an animal to be fossilized is that it must be buried in a depositional area: that is, more and more layers of mud or gravel must be laid down over it. If the area is subject to erosion—and nearly all land surfaces are—the fossil will soon be washed out and destroyed.

The third step is that this depositional area must at some time become an erosional area, so that wind and water wear it down and uncover the buried remains.

The fourth step necessary for the recovery of a fossil is that when the fossil is uncovered, someone knowledgeable has to walk along that ridge, or study the face of that cliff, and locate the fossil and recover it. The time frame for this recovery varies, but it is always short. The fossil is protected until it is exposed, but it also is invisible. As soon as it is exposed, wind and water attack it, and they can destroy it quickly. The best fossils are found when someone spots an exposed bone that turns out to be part of a buried skeleton, and therefore still well preserved. But many fine fossils have been washed away because no one happened to see them when they were first exposed, or the people who saw them didn't realize what they were seeing.

And as if that were not enough, even the processes of evolution contribute to the lack of transitional fossils the creationists love to cite. Evolutionary changes tend to occur in small, isolated communities, and the new animals then move into the general territory and supplant their relatives there. The transition seems to be abrupt everywhere except the small area where the change occurred. And we seldom are lucky enough to find those small areas where the changes occurred, even if they were fossilized.

The famed Morrison Basin

Geologists call a distinctive body of rock that serves as a convenient unit for study and mapping a "formation," and name it for some spot where it is exposed. The problems and rewards of the fossil record are well illustrated by the Morrison Formation, named for a small town in the Front Range just west of Denver where it crops out. It was formed in the late Jurassic period, around 150,000,000 years ago, in the Morrison Basin, a vast subtropical area that extended from central New Mexico north to Saskatchewan. It covered about 750,000 square miles, including north-eastern Arizona, eastern Utah, Colorado, northwestern Kansas, western Nebraska, Wyoming, most of Montana and more than half of North and South Dakota, plus small corners of Texas, Oklahoma, Idaho, Manitoba, and Alberta. It was a hot, humid area of meandering streams and tangled forests, with seasonal dry spells. It was a dinosaur paradise.

When the first dinosaur fossil hunters came west in the 1870s, many of the great deposits they found were in the Morrison Formation. Cañon City, Colorado, and Como Bluff and Bone Cabin, Wyoming, were among the early quarries that produced wonders people had never seen before: huge sauropods including the camarasaurs, apatosaurs and long diplodocuses, and the gigantic brachiosaurs; strange stegosaurs with their double row of plates down their backs, and the carnivores that preyed on them, allosaurs and ceratosaurs. Later sites of finds include Dinosaur National Monument, Utah, where many corpses piled up on a sandbar in a sluggish river, and the Cleveland-Lloyd quarry in central Utah. This was a predator trap where five or six huge sauropods got stuck in a mud hole, drawing hundreds of carnivores, which in turn got stuck in the mud and added to the carrion smell, which drew more carnivores.

More recent finds in the Morrison Formation include the Dry Mesa quarry in western Colorado, which produced the super giants ultrasaurus and supersaurus, and the seismosaur site in New Mexico, where much of a diplodocus-related animal up to 140 feet long was lodged on a sandbar.

What a productive stratum! It has given us a large part of what we know about the late Jurassic plants and animals.

The creationists' emphasis on the gaps of the fossil record is just another example of the nit-picking they do to try to cover their lack of evidence.

But nearly all of the eastern half of the Morrison Formation is still buried under the prairies of the high plains. Most of the quarries are west of the Front Range in Colorado, and the Rocky Mountain uplift has destroyed much of the Morrison. It has been stripped off of the Colorado mountains, the San Rafael Swell in Utah, and many other areas including the Black Hills. The Colorado River has washed it away in the canyonlands of Utah and northern Arizona. The Rio Grande rift has cut a swath through it. Volcanic action in the Yellowstone area has destroyed it in that region.

The present-day map of the Morrison Formation, reveals that about 75 percent of it is still buried, and nearly all of the rest is washed out and destroyed. That portion of the Morrison Formation available to paleontologists—the part that has produced the wonders described above—appears to be about one percent of the total formation, perhaps less.

But those pieces we do have of this Morrison puzzle form a coherent whole. Of course parts are missing, but just as the public library's collection of books is incomplete but still gives a good picture of modern civilization, so too do those parts of the Morrison formation corroborate and extend each other to give a good broad overview of life at that time and place. Camarasaurs and allosaurs are found in all areas. The Cleveland-

Lloyd quarry gave us new carnivores, like stokesosaur and marshosaur, to go with the allosaurs and ceratosaurs. Dry Mesa gave us another big predator, torvosaur. And the finds are continuing: workers at Dinosaur National Monument in recent years turned up a nearly complete theropod (unfortunately missing the head) they have been calling "not an allosaur," which had a furcula, like a bird's wishbone, intact in the skeleton. Paleontologists in Cañon City are preparing a beautifully preserved and nearly complete skeleton of a stegosaur. Utah workers are excavating a camarasaur at Mussentuchit Wash, southwest of the San Rafael Swell.

The outline is there

We are never going to have a complete picture of Morrison life. We're not going to strip thousands of feet of overburden off the high plains! But we don't have to do that to have a good, broad understanding of what life was like in Morrison time. Since the quarries are in different levels of the Morrison Formation, representing different parts of Morrison time, we even have a good grasp for the way the animals evolved through time.

And that understanding is more real, more valuable and much more profound than anything the creationists could ever acquire with their all-or-nothing insistence on some impossible ideal world.

It's not true that, "If we don't know everything, we don't know anything!" We know a lot about the Morrison Formation and the thousands of formations that make up this wonderful world. We are missing some details, but the broad outlines are clear. And new finds are adding to our knowledge every day. That's where the fun is; that's what keeps the fossil hunters wandering the ridges looking for those little telltale scraps of bone.

The creationists' emphasis on the gaps of the fossil record is just another example of the nit-picking they do to try to cover their lack of evidence. They do not share science's commitment to a free and open search for truth. Since they have no facts to present, creationists are reduced to searching for debater's tricks to try to shore up their arguments, including the absurdity that evidence against "evolution"—that is, against biology and geology—is somehow evidence for their position. In so doing, they miss the reality, and the drama and excitement and fun, of the history of life on this fantastic planet.

10

Evolution by Design Succeeds Where Darwin Fails

Jonathan Wells

*Jonathan Wells holds doctorates in both biology (University of Califor-
nia at Berkeley) and theology (Yale). When he wrote this article, he was
a postdoctoral research biologist in the Department of Molecular and
Cell Biology, University of California, Berkeley, and a fellow of the Discovery Institute in Seattle.*

Evolutionary biologists reject the idea of design in evolution. They
fully support Darwin's concept of natural selection, which implies
that change is governed by chance alone. Yet the evidence
demonstrates that Darwin's theory cannot be reconciled with several important features of evolution. Therefore, it appears that
Darwin's naturalistic explanation for the history of life has wide-
spread acceptance among evolutionary biologists for one reason:
The alternative, conscious design, is completely unacceptable.

Before the twentieth century, most Western scientists believed that
God created living things by design. Belief in God was part of the very
fabric of Western civilization; and by viewing the world through the spec-
tacles of faith, people saw it as God's handiwork. In the words of John
Henry Newman, "I believe in design because I believe in God; not in a
God because I see design."

In the eighteenth and nineteenth centuries, however, some thinkers
reversed the traditional logic to argue from design to God's existence.
William Paley wrote in *Natural Theology* (1802) that someone crossing a
heath and finding a watch would see that "its several parts are framed and
put together for a purpose" and would conclude that it had been designed
by a watchmaker. Analogously, Paley argued, one could conclude that living things are designed by God.

Darwin's exclusion of design

Charles Darwin was born into this intellectual environment in 1809. By the time his *Origin of Species* was published in 1859, Darwin had become convinced that the design that Paley claimed to see in living things was an illusion. According to Darwin, what appears to be design in living things can be explained naturalistically as the result of random variations and natural selection. [In this essay, "naturalism" and "naturalistic" refer to the philosophical doctrine that the physical universe is the whole of reality and that ideas and the supernatural are human projections.]

Darwin argued that just as domestic livestock can be modified by selecting certain variants for breeding, so wild species are modified by a "natural selection" due to competition for survival. According to Darwin, the continuation of such "descent with modification" over millions of years produced all living things from one or a few original organisms. He saw no room for design in this process. When Harvard botanist Asa Gray proposed that God had designed the variations on which natural selection operated, Darwin rejected the idea and concluded his 1868 *Variation of Animals and Plants Under Domestication* with a refutation of design. According to Darwin, the products of random variation and natural selection cannot be regarded as designed; and human beings, as the latest in a long series of undesigned results, are the least designed of all.

Darwin's modern followers concur. In 1967, paleontologist George Gaylord Simpson wrote: "Man is the result of a purposeless and natural process that did not have him in mind" *(The Meaning of Evolution,* revised edition). In 1970, molecular biologist and Nobel laureate Jacques Monod announced that "the mechanism of Darwinism is at last securely founded," and thus "man has to understand that he is a mere accident" (quoted in H.F. Judson's *The Eighth Day of Creation,* 1979). And in 1986, zoologist Richard Dawkins wrote a best-selling book titled *The Blind Watchmaker: Why the Evidence of Evolution Reveals a Universe Without Design.*

According to Darwin, what appears to be design in living things can be explained naturalistically as the result of random variations and natural selection.

But the "evidence" that Dawkins cites in *The Blind Watchmaker* consists almost entirely of computer simulations. He argues that Darwinism would have to be true even if there were no evidence for it, because short of postulating the existence of a deity (which Dawkins rejects), Darwin's theory of "*cumulative selection,* by slow and gradual degrees, is . . . the only workable explanation that has ever been proposed, for the existence of life's complex design." In other words, what persuades Dawkins that Darwinian evolution is true is not the evidence, but the fact that it is the only tenable naturalistic explanation for the history of life. As he writes in the book's opening chapter, "Darwin made it possible to be an intellectually fulfilled atheist."

Evolutionary biologists are virtually unanimous in their rejection of design, though some (such as paleontologist Stephen Jay Gould) sharply disagree with Dawkins over the sufficiency of Darwin's mechanism of gradual selection. Yet if one wishes to exclude design on scientific grounds, one must do so on the basis of a demonstrated mechanism; mere descent with modification is not enough. This point is unintentionally illustrated by biologist Tim Berra in *Evolution and the Myth of Creationism* (1990):

> If you look at a 1953 Corvette and compare it to the latest model, only the most general resemblances are evident, but if you compare a 1953 and a 1954 Corvette, side by side, then a 1954 and a 1955 model, and so on, the descent with modification is overwhelmingly obvious. This is what paleontologists do with fossils, *and the evidence is so solid and comprehensive that it cannot be denied by reasonable people.*

But the historical development of the Corvette, which Berra calls "descent with modification," is undeniably due to construction according to pre-existing plans—that is, design. Ironically, therefore, his analogy shows that descent with modification is compatible with design.

Evidence has been accumulating for decades, however, that Darwin's mechanism fails to account for major features of evolution. The fossil record (especially where it is most complete) lacks the innumerable transitional forms that Darwin's theory predicts; artificial breeding (no matter how intense or protracted) fails to produce the major modifications that his theory requires; and embryonic development (as revealed by modern comparative embryology) is radically different from Darwinian expectations. According to molecular biologist Michael Denton (*Evolution: A Theory in Crisis*, 1986), not "one single empirical discovery or scientific advance since 1859" has validated Darwin's theory that large-scale evolution is caused by natural selection acting on random variations.

Given the empirical anomalies, and the sharp disagreement over mechanism between Dawkins and Gould, it is clear that the modern Darwinian denial of design rests on nonempirical grounds. It is no longer an inference from evidence but an a priori assumption based on a commitment to naturalistic philosophy.

Reintroducing design

One good metaphysical a priori deserves another. Since Darwinists have shifted their ground from science to philosophy, it is legitimate to ask whether their axiomatic exclusion of design is the only logical possibility. The answer, obviously, is no. Before Darwin, design was taken for granted by most Western scientists, and even today, a significant number of scientists view the world as designed.

For the remainder of this paper, I will assume that living things are designed—not necessarily in every detail, but in at least certain aspects. Specifically, I will assume that the human species was planned before life began and that the history of life is the record of how this plan was implemented.

The Darwinian account of the history of life begins with the most primitive organisms and works its way forward to the appearance of human beings. Although this is how events actually unfolded, from a design perspective the idea of human beings came first, followed by a plan to achieve the goal. In a sense, then, the plan took shape by working backward from the goal.[1]

What would the plan have to include? Any plan that places humans as the intended outcome would have to provide for such basic needs as food, water, and a suitable environment. It can be argued that humans have other needs as well, including social interactions, intellectual stimulation, and aesthetic enjoyment. Here I will focus entirely on physical needs.

When human beings first appeared, the environment must have been congenial to unprotected human life. From a design perspective, this human-friendly environment was planned. Advocates of the Anthropic Principle have pointed out that such an environment was possible only because the fundamental physical constants of the universe had the precise values they have. But these constants are consistent with a wide range of environments, whereas life requires a relatively narrow range of temperature, pressure, and other physical parameters. Therefore, in addition to the universal constants, suitable local conditions would have needed to be part of the design as well.

Evidence has been accumulating for decades, however, that Darwin's mechanism fails to account for major features of evolution.

Humans use oxygen in their metabolism and release carbon dioxide as a waste product. Therefore, suitable local conditions must include an atmosphere containing these gases and a mechanism that regenerates oxygen from carbon dioxide. This mechanism is photosynthesis, which is carried out by green plants. It uses energy from the sun and also produces carbohydrates—another raw material in human metabolism.

Photosynthesis is a remarkably efficient system for maintaining an environment congenial to human life. Unless some other mechanism is shown to be capable of fulfilling the same role, a design perspective implies that organisms very much like green plants were a necessary part of the original plan.

In addition to carbohydrates, the human body needs various other nutrients, including specific amino acids, minerals, and vitamins. Our nutritional needs are quite complex and must be met on a regular basis, so we are absolutely dependent on a variety of food sources. These are found in the plants and animals around us. Since our needs include complex organic molecules found only in other living things, those organisms are necessary for our existence.

Whatever organisms may have been necessary for human nutrition, their existence required a balanced ecosystem that accommodated their needs. The original plan must have included a self-sustaining biosphere in which reproduction and growth were balanced by death and decay. The balance among organisms in an ecosystem is normally quite complex, and ecologists frequently discover that organisms previously thought to be unessential are necessary elements in that balance. It is thus clear that planning for human beings requires planning for many other organisms as well.

Getting from there to here

The need for large numbers of organisms becomes even more evident when we try to imagine how human beings appeared on what was originally a lifeless planet. Although there is no consensus among paleogeologists about atmospheric conditions on the primitive earth, those conditions were almost certainly different from today's. The first organisms must have been capable of surviving in those conditions and transforming them into an environment more favorable to human life.

In other words, primitive organisms had to pave the way for the stable ecosystems we see today. A barren planet had to become a garden; soils containing organic nutrients for land plants had to be produced. To use current biological terminology, ecological niches were filled by organisms adapted to survive under local conditions. Those organisms then transformed their conditions, and other living things took over.

Producing a congenial environment with nutritious foods, while necessary, would not have been sufficient. Some people believe that the first human beings were created fully grown. But even if we ignore psychological considerations and restrict ourselves to physical ones, birth and growth are essential aspects of human beings as we know them. A creature that begins life without passing through birth and childhood would be so unlike us that we could not regard it as truly human, regardless of how great the superficial resemblance. And because human babies are totally dependent on other creatures for their survival during early development, animals capable of raising the first human babies must have been a necessary part of the original plan.

Human babies need milk to survive and grow, so mammals had to exist before humans appeared. And not just any mammal. The first human baby presumably had to be nurtured by a creature very much like itself—a humanlike primate. This creature, in turn, could only have been nurtured by a creature intermediate in some respects between it and a more primitive mammal. In other words, a plan for the emergence of human beings must have included something like the succession of prehistoric forms we find in the fossil record.

A design perspective on the history of life might turn out to account for the biological evidence better than Darwinian evolution can.

Similar reasoning could be applied to earlier episodes in the history of life. For example, just as mammals were necessary predecessors of the first humans, mammallike reptiles were presumably needed to precede the first mammals, and so on. The emergence of humans thus depended on a progression of creatures that increasingly resembled us.

Although this process is superficially similar to the Darwinian notion of common descent, design theory differs from the latter in maintaining that predecessors need not be biological ancestors but only providers of essential nourishment and protection. Successive organisms are "related" in the sense that they represent planned stages in the history of life, but they are not genetically related as ancestors and descendants. A planned succession would not require the innumerable transitional forms that Darwin predicted. Design theory is thus more compatible than Darwinism with the discontinuities found in the fossil record.

Design theory also does a better job than Darwin's theory in accounting for homology. According to Darwin, features in diverse organisms are structurally similar ("homologous") because they are inherited from a common ancestor. Biological inheritance implies that such features are more similar because they are produced by similar genes or developmental pathways, but this implication is contradicted by the genetic and embryological evidence.[2] In a design view, however, homologies exist (at least in part) because new organisms need to be protected and nourished by organisms somewhat like them. But homologies need not be produced by similar genes or developmental pathways, since there is no insistence on the sort of mechanistic continuity required by Darwinian common descent.

In conclusion, a design perspective on the history of life might turn out to account for the biological evidence better than Darwinian evolution can. For example, Darwinism fails to specify why any given organism exists, beyond insisting that it be able to survive. But for design theory, a variety of creatures—including green plants and humanlike primates—are necessary prerequisites for human life. A design perspective requires progressive stages in the history of life, as seen in the fossil record, but unlike Darwin's theory it does not predict innumerable transitional forms that do not exist. Design theory also suggests that homologies exist, at least in part, so that certain organisms can prepare the way for others intended to follow them. Unlike Darwinism, it does not imply that homologous features are produced by similar genes or developmental pathways, and so does not run afoul of the evidence.

This analysis, although preliminary and subject to revision, demonstrates that a design perspective has major implications for our understanding of the biological evidence. As our knowledge of ecology and human physiology increases, and as the analysis is refined and expanded, more detailed implications will follow. In this way, a design perspective may eventually provide a detailed account of the history of life more faithful to the evidence than Darwin's theory and thus offer a framework for more fruitful research programs in biology.

Notes

1. See Unification Thought Institute, *From Evolution Theory to a New Creation Theory: Errors in Darwinism and a Proposal From Unification Thought* (Tokyo: Kogensha, 1996).

2. See Jonathan Wells, "Homology in Biology: A Problem for Naturalistic Science," presented at the Conference on Naturalism, Theism, and the Scientific Enterprise, Department of Philosophy, University of Texas, Austin, February 1997 (posted on the World Wide Web at http://www.dla.utexas.edu/depts/philosophy/faculty/koons/ntse/papers/Wells.html).

11

Evolution Is Consistent with Belief in God

Kenneth R. Miller

Kenneth R. Miller, a recipient of numerous awards for outstanding teaching, is a cell biologist, a professor of biology at Brown University, and the co-author of widely used high school and college biology textbooks. He is a regular contributor to scientific journals and magazines, including Nature, Scientific American, *and* Cell.

Religion has been forced to alter and modify its view of God to conform to the tenets of biological evolution. Therefore creationists feel compelled to attack evolutionary theory in order to free the Creator from its shackles. However, religion in general and God in particular need not be subordinated to the findings of evolutionary biology. Rather, evolution provides a much more meaningful and poignant explanation of the relationship of the Creator to his creation.

The displacement of God by Darwinian forces in this century is now almost complete. We no longer explain the specializations of an animal or the multiple levels of a food chain in terms of how they fit into God's will, but seek instead to understand the natural forces that shaped each of them over time. As a result, the way in which we appreciate the natural world has changed forever, almost exactly as Charles Darwin had anticipated:

> When the views advanced by me in this volume . . . or when analogous views on the origin of species are generally admitted, we can dimly foresee that there will be a considerable revolution in natural history. . . .

> When we no longer look at an organic being as a savage looks at a ship, as at something wholly beyond his comprehension; when we regard every production of nature as one which has had a history; when we contemplate every complex structure and instinct as the summing up of many con-

trivances, each useful to the possessor, nearly in the same way as when we look at any great mechanical invention as the summing up of the labour, the experience, the reason, and even the blunders of numerous workmen; when we thus view each organic being, how far more interesting, I speak from experience, will the study of natural history become![1]

Well, the views contained within *The Origin* have now been "generally admitted," and the study of natural history has indeed become, as Darwin understated it, "far more interesting." Together with the other makers of modern scientific reality, Darwin lifted the curtain that allowed us to see the world as it really is. And to any person of faith, this should mean that Charles Darwin ultimately brought us closer to an understanding of God.

Darwin's fears

Darwin himself clearly worried that he had done exactly the opposite. Desmond and Moore, whose excellent biography of Darwin describes these doubts and fears, concluded a stirring summary of the events surrounding Darwin's death and burial in Westminster Abbey with these lines:

Darwin's body was enshrined to the greater glory of the new professionals who had snatched it. The burial was their apotheosis, the last rite of a rising secularity. It marked the accession to power of the traders in nature's marketplace, the scientists and their minions in politics and religion. Such men, on the up-and-up, were paying their dues, for Darwin had naturalized Creation and delivered human nature and human destiny into their hands.

Society would never be the same. The "Devil's Chaplain" has done his work.[2]

Which is it? Did Darwin contribute to the greater glory of God, or did he deliver human nature and destiny into the hands of a professional scientific class, one profoundly hostile to religion? Darwin's own views on the subject are so complex and ambiguous that they offer little help. At one time, he said that "agnostic would be the most correct description of my state of mind";[3] but at another, he wrote that he was overwhelmed by

the extreme difficulty, or rather the impossibility, of conceiving this immense and wonderful universe, including man with his capacity for looking far backwards and far into futurity, as the result of blind chance or necessity. When thus reflecting I feel compelled to look to a First Cause having an intelligent mind in some degree analogous to that of man; and I deserve to be called a Theist.[4]

Cementing his reputation as a fence-sitter, in *The Origin* Darwin took special care to take neither position, declaring his work religiously neutral:

I see no good reason why the views given in this volume should shock the religious feelings of any one. It is satisfactory, as showing how transient such impressions are, to remember that the greatest discovery ever made by man, namely, the law of the attraction of gravity, was also attacked by Leibnitz, "as subversive of natural and inferentially revealed, religion." A celebrated author and divine has written to me that "he has gradually learnt to see that is it just as noble a conception of the Deity to believe that He created a few original forms capable of self-development into other and needful forms, as to believe that He required a fresh act of creation to supply the voids caused by the actions of His laws."[5]

Darwin, significantly, presented this expansive "conception of the Deity" only as the idea of another, keeping his own views guarded. His cautious language may have been the result of genuine conviction, or could have been intended, as some biographers have written, to spare his family social embarrassment. No matter. The importance of what Darwin has done rises or falls on its own merits, and not on his personal intentions, hopes, or fears. What matters to us today is whether Darwin's work strengthens or weakens the idea of God, whether it serves to enlarge or to diminish a theistic view of the world.

Evolution's effect on religion

The conventional wisdom is that, whatever one may think of his science, having Mr. Darwin around certainly hasn't helped religion very much. The general thinking is that religion has been weakened by Darwinism, and has been constrained to modify its view of the Creator in order to twist doctrine into conformance with the demands of evolution. As a result, even if we were generous enough to accept science *and* religion as co-equal ways of knowing, Orwellian common sense would tell us that one of these partners is more equal than the other. Much more equal. As Stephen Jay Gould puts it, with obvious delight,

> Now the conclusions of science must be accepted *a priori*, and religious interpretations must be finessed and adjusted to match unimpeachable results from the magisterium of natural knowledge![6]

Science calls the tune, and religion dances to its music.

Even the most fervent atheists will stipulate that one can apologize a theistic vision, with due retrospective care, onto almost any scientific reality. This makes God a pesky and elusive target, hard to pin down and impossible to exclude. Nonetheless, to absolute materialists it also means that the aftermath of Darwin is a diminished, roundabout, apologetic version of belief in which religion must constantly be modified to the demands of the scientific moment.

This sad specter of God, weakened and marginalized, drives the continuing opposition to evolution. This is why the God of the creationists requires, above all else, that evolution be shown not to have functioned in the past and not to be working now. To free religion from the tyranny of Darwinism, their only hope is to require that science show nature to be incomplete, and that key events in the history of life can only be explained as the result of supernatural processes. Put bluntly, the creationists are committed to finding permanent, intractable mystery in nature. To such minds, even the most perfect being we can imagine still wouldn't be perfect enough to have fashioned a creation in which life would originate and evolve on its own. The nature they require science to discover is one that is flawed, static, and forever inadequate.

This sad specter of God, weakened and marginalized, drives the continuing opposition to evolution.

Science in general, and evolutionary science in particular, give us something quite different. Through them we see a universe that is dynamic, flexible, and logically complete. They present a vision of life that spreads across the planet with endless variety and intricate beauty. They suggest a world in which our material existence is not an impossible illusion propped up by magic, but the genuine article, a world in which things are exactly what they seem, in which we were formed, as the Creator once cared to tell us, from the dust of the earth itself.

Evolution and freedom

It is often said that a Darwinian universe is one in which the random collisions of particles govern all events and therefore the world is without meaning. I disagree. A world without meaning would be one in which a Deity pulled the string of every human puppet, and every material particle as well. In such a world, physical and biological events would be carefully controlled, evil and suffering could be minimized, and the outcome of historical processes strictly regulated. All things would move towards the Creator's clear, distinct, established goals. Those who find discomfort in evolution often say that lack of such certainty in the outcome of Darwin's relentless scheme of natural history shows that it could not be reconciled with their faith. Maybe so. But certainty of outcome means that control and predictability come at the price of independence. By being always in control, the Creator would deny His creatures any real opportunity to know and worship Him. Authentic love requires freedom, not manipulation. Such freedom is best supplied by the open contingency of evolution, and not by strings of divine direction attached to every living creature.

The common view that religion must tiptoe around the findings of evolutionary biology is simply and plainly wrong.

One hundred and fifty years ago it might have been impossible not to couple Darwin with a grim and pointless determinism. I believe this is why Darwin in his later years tried and failed to find God, at least a God consistent with his theories. If organisms were mechanisms, and mechanisms were driven only by the physics and chemistry of nature, then we humans were trapped in a material world in which past and future were interlocked in mindless certainty. In such a world, the only chance for God's action would have been in the construction of organisms themselves. Darwin surely felt he had denied himself that refuge by accounting for the illusion of design. As a result, he may well have felt, despite his unwillingness to admit to a world produced by "blind chance or necessity," that he had ruled out any realistic possibility for God. That his God could never be found.

God and evolution

Things look different today. Darwin's vision has expanded to encompass a new world of biology in which the links from molecule to cell and from cell to organism are becoming clear. Evolution prevails, but it prevails with a richness and subtlety its originator may have found surprising, and in the context of developments in other sciences he could not have anticipated.

We know from astronomy that the universe had a beginning, from physics that the future is both open and unpredictable, from geology and paleontology that the whole of life has been a process of change and transformation. From biology we know that our tissues are not impenetrable reservoirs of vital magic, but a stunning matrix of complex wonders, ultimately explicable in terms of biochemistry and molecular biology. With such knowledge we can see, perhaps for the first time, why a Creator would have allowed our species to be fashioned by the process of evolution.

If he so chose, the God whose presence is taught by most Western religions could have fashioned anything, ourselves included, *ex nihilo*, from his wish alone. In our childhood as a species, that might have been the only way in which we could imagine the fulfillment of His will. But we've grown up, and something remarkable has happened—we have begun to understand the physical basis of life itself. If the persistence of life were beyond the capabilities of matter, if a string of constant miracles were needed for each turn of the cell cycle or each flicker of a cilium, the hand of God would be written directly into every living thing—His presence at the edge of the human sandbox would be unmistakable. Such findings might confirm our faith, but they would also undermine our independence. How could we fairly choose between God and man when the presence and the power of the divine so obviously and so literally controlled our every breath? Our freedom as His creatures requires a little space, some integrity, a consistency and self-sufficiency to the material world.

The common view that religion must tiptoe around the findings of evolutionary biology is simply and plainly wrong.

Accepting evolution is neither more nor less than the result of respecting the reality and consistency of the physical world over time. We are material beings with an independent physical existence, and to fashion such beings, any Creator would have had to produce an independent material universe in which our evolution over time was a contingent possibility. A believer in the divine accepts that God's love and His gifts of freedom are genuine—so genuine that they include the power to choose evil and, if we wish, to freely send ourselves to hell. Not all believers will accept the stark conditions of that bargain, but our freedom to act has to have a physical and biological basis. Evolution and its sister sciences of genetics and molecular biology provide that basis. A biologically static world would leave a Creator's creatures with neither freedom nor the independence required to exercise that freedom. In biological terms, evolution is the only way a Creator could have made us the creatures we are—free beings in a world of authentic and meaningful moral and spiritual choices.

In biological terms, evolution is the only way a Creator could have made us the creatures we are— free beings in a world of authentic and meaningful moral and spiritual choices.

Those who ask from science a final argument, an ultimate proof, an unassailable position from which the issue of God may be decided, will always be disappointed. As a scientist I claim no new proofs, no revolutionary data, no stunning insight into nature that can tip the balance in one direction or another. But I do claim that to a believer, even in the most traditional sense, evolutionary biology is not at all the obstacle we often believe it to be. In many respects, evolution is the key to understanding our relationship with God. God's physical intervention in our lives is not direct. But His care and love are constants, and the strength He gives, while the stuff of miracle, is a miracle of hope, faith, and inspiration.

Notes

1. C. Darwin, *The Origin of Species* (6th ed.). London: Oxford University Press, 1956, pp. 555–57.

2. A. Desmond and J. Moore, *Darwin: The Life of a Tormented Evolutionist*. New York: Warner Books, 1991, p. 677.

3. Ibid, p. 636. Original quote from his 1879 autobiography, p. 29.

4. F. Darwin (ed.), *Life and Letters of Charles Darwin*. New York: D. Appleton, 1887, p. 282.

5. Darwin, *The Origin*, pp. 550–51.

6. S.J. Gould, *Rock of Ages*. New York: Ballantine Publishing, 1999, p. 213.

Organizations to Contact

The editors have compiled the following list of organizations concerned with the issues debated in this book. The descriptions are derived from material provided by the organizations. All have publications or information available for interested readers. The list was compiled on the date of publication of the present volume; the information provided here may change. Be aware that many organizations take several weeks or longer to respond to inquiries so allow as much time as possible.

American Scientific Affiliation (ASA)
PO Box 668, Ipswich, MA 01938
(978) 356-5656 • fax: (978) 356-4375
e-mail: asa@asa3.org

ASA membership is composed of industrial and academic scientists subscribing to the Christian faith. It seeks to integrate, communicate, and facilitate properly researched science and biblical theology in service to the Church and the science community. It seeks to have theology and science interacting in a positive light. Its publications include the *American Scientific Affiliation Newsletter* and *Perspectives on Science and Christian Faith*.

Creation Research Society (CRS)
PO Box 8263, St. Joseph, MO 64508-8263
e-mail: CRSnetwork@aol.com

Persons with at least a master's degree in some branch of science are voting members, and sustaining members are other interested individuals. CRS is for Christians who believe that the facts of science support the revealed account of creation in the Bible. It maintains a laboratory-equipped research center in Arizona (see below) and conducts research and disseminates information to the public.

Creation Research Society (CRS)
Van Andel Research Center
6801 North Hwy. 89, Chino Valley, AZ 86323
(520) 636-1153 • fax: (520) 636-1153
e-mail: crsvarc@primenet.com

CRS facilitates and supports the scientific study of the theories of creation and evolution. Its resources include a meteor astronomy observatory, research greenhouse, electronics lab, gas chromatograph, and virtual instrumentation. Its publications include *Creation Research Society Quarterly*.

Genesis Institute (GI)
740 South 128th St., Seattle, WA 98168-2728
e-mail: whjl@juno.com

GI is made up of individuals seeking to publicize the value of the Gospel in sciences and bring the Bible and science together. It stresses Creation Evangelism and believes that the universe is less than six thousand years old. It conducts educational and research programs and offers home schooling services.

Institute for Creation Research (ICR)
10946 Woodside Ave., Suite N, Santee, CA 92071
(619) 448-0900 • fax: (619) 448-3469
website: www.icr.org

ICR asserts the inerrancy of Scripture through the abundant evidence in science. It conducts research and education. Its publications include *Acts and Facts, Days of Praise.* Its educational activities include summer institutes, educational workshops, graduate school courses, lectures, and seminar programs.

Institute of Human Origins (IHO)
Arizona State University
PO Box 874101, Tempe, AZ 85287-4101
(480) 727-6508 • fax: (480) 727-6570
e-mail: iho@asu.edu

The institute is comprised of scientists, educators, students, volunteers, and other individuals carrying out or supporting research on human evolution. It utilizes the expertise and knowledge of many disciplines to establish when, where, and how the human species originated. It promotes laboratory and field research. It provides a base from which research can be pursued from the planning stages to the dissemination of results. It offers specialized training to scientists and students and maintains a repository and data center of photos, slides, casts, field notes, and comparative collections. It compiles statistics and maintains a speakers' bureau.

National Academy of Sciences (NAS)
2101 Constitution Ave. NW, Washington, DC 20418
(202) 334-2000 • fax: (202) 334-2158
website: www.nas.edu

The NAS is a private, honorary organization dedicated to furthering of science and engineering; members are elected in recognition of their distinguished and continuing contributions to either of the two fields. Founded by an act of Congress to serve as official adviser to the federal government on scientific and technical matters. Its publications include *Biographical Memoirs* and the monthly *Proceedings of the National Academy of Sciences.*

National Center for Science Education (NCSE)
925 Kearney St., El Cerrito, CA 94530-2810
(800) 290-6006 • (510) 526-1674 • fax: (510) 526-1675
e-mail: ncse@natcenscied.org • website: www.natcenscied.org

NCSE is affiliated with the American Association for the Advancement of Science. It is made up of scientists, teachers, students, clergy, and interested individuals. NCSE seeks to improve science education, specifically the study of evolutionary science, and opposes the teaching of creationism as part of public school science curricula. It publishes books, pamphlets, and audio and videocassettes on evolution education and education on the nature of scientific inquiry. It also publishes *Reports of the National Center for Science Education.* It reaches markets through direct mail and accepts unsolicited manuscripts on evolution and science education.

National Science Teachers Association (NSTA)
1840 Wilson Blvd., Arlington, VA 22201-3000
(703) 243-7100 • fax: (703) 243-7177
e-mail: publicinfo@nsta.org • website: www.nsta.org

NSTA is made up of teachers seeking to foster excellence in science teaching. It studies students and how they learn, the curriculum of science, the teacher and his/her preparation, the procedures used in classroom and laboratory, the facilities for teaching science, and the evaluation procedures used. Its publications include *Journal of College Science Teaching, Reports on the Teaching of Science at the College Level*. It also publishes curriculum development and professional materials, teaching aids, career booklets, and audiovisual aids.

Reasons to Believe (RTB)
PO Box 5978, Pasadena, CA 91117
(800) 482-7836 • (626) 335-1480 • fax: (626) 852-0178
e-mail: reasons@reasons.org • website: www.reasons.org/

RTB seeks to explain the theory of creation in a biblically sound and scientifically valid manner, in an effort to remove the doubts of skeptics and strengthen the faith of Christians. It conducts research and educational programs and operates a speakers' bureau. Its publications include the quarterly newsletter, *Facts and Faith*.

Bibliography

Books

Peter W. Atkins — *Creation Revisited.* New York: W.H. Freeman, 1992.

Walter Brown — *In the Beginning: Compelling Evidence for Creation and the Flood.* Phoenix, AZ: Center for Scientific Creation, 1996.

Paul Davies — *The Mind of God: The Scientific Basis for a Rational World.* New York: Simon and Schuster, 1992.

Richard Dawkins — *The Blind Watchmaker: Why the Evidence of Evolution Reveals a Universe Without Design.* New York: W.W. Norton, 1987.

Richard Dawkins — *Climbing Mount Improbable.* New York: W.W. Norton, 1997.

Daniel C. Dennett — *Darwin's Dangerous Idea: Evolution and the Meaning of Life.* New York: Simon and Schuster, 1995.

Michael Denton — *Evolution: A Theory in Crisis.* Bethesda, MD: Adler and Adler, 1985.

Ronald L. Ecker — *Dictionary of Science and Creationism.* Buffalo, NY: Prometheus Books, 1990.

John F. Haught — *God After Darwin: A Theology of Evolution.* Boulder, CO: Westview Press, 2000.

John Horgan — *The End of Science.* Reading, MA: Addison-Wesley, 1996.

Phillip E. Johnson — *Defeating Darwinism by Opening Minds.* Downers Grove, IL: InterVarsity Press, 1997.

Stuart A. Kauffman — *At Home in the Universe: The Search for the Laws of Self-Organization and Complexity.* New York: Oxford University Press, 1995.

Richard Milton — *Shattering the Myths of Darwinism.* Rochester, VT: Park Street Press, 1997.

Seyyed Hossein Nasr — *Religion and the Order of Nature.* New York: Oxford University Press, 1996.

Ronald L. Numbers — *The Creationists: The Evolution of Scientific Creationism.* New York: Alfred A. Knopf, 1992.

Michael Ruse, ed. — *But Is It Science? The Philosophical Question in the Creation/Evolution Controversy.* Buffalo, NY: Prometheus Books, 1996.

Gerald Schroeder — *The Science of God: The Convergence of Scientific and Biblical Wisdom.* New York: Broadway Books, 1998.

Lee Tiffin	*Creationism's Upside-Down Pyramid: How Science Refutes Fundamentalism*. Buffalo, NY: Prometheus Books, 1994.
Jonathan Weiner	*The Beak of the Finch: A Story of Evolution in Our Time*. New York: W.A. Knopf, 1994.

Periodicals

Larry Arnhart	"Darwin's Science of Morality," *American Outlook*, November/December 2000.
Michael J. Behe	"Darwin's Hostages," *American Spectator*, December 1999/January 2000.
T. Bethell	"The Evolution Wars," *American Spectator*, December 1999/January 2000.
Colleen Carroll	"Evolution of a Creationist Victory," *National Catholic Reporter*, October 8, 1999.
Mona Charen	"Scopes Trial Replayed in Kansas," *Conservative Chronicle*, August 25, 1999.
William A. Dembski	"Shamelessly Doubting Darwin," *American Outlook*, November/December 2000.
Dennis Duehning	"ACLU Trashes 'Politically Incorrect' Christian Teacher," *Life Advocate*, November/December 1998.
Thomas J. Geelan	"When Creationism Goes to School," *Free Inquiry*, Spring 2000.
John Gibeart	"Evolution of Controversy," *ABA Journal*, November 1999.
Stanley L. Jaki	"The Biblical Basis of Western Science," *Crisis*, October 1997.
Phillip Johnson	"What's the Problem with Teaching Evolution When There's So Much Evidence for It?" *Moody*, March/April 1999.
Donald Kaul	"Creationists' Idolatry: Making God in Their Own Image," *Liberal Opinion Week*, September 20, 1999.
Wendy Kramer	"Are We Evolved Yet?" *Free Inquiry*, Fall 2000.
Paul Kurtz	"Darwin Re-Crucified," *Free Inquiry*, Spring 1998.
Thomas Lessl	"Darwinism, Dawkinism, and Christian Accommodation," *New Oxford Review*, February 2000.
Molleen Matsumura	"How to Fight Creationist/Evolutionist Battles," *Free Inquiry*, Spring 1998.
Stephen C. Meyer	"DNA and Other Designs," *First Things*, April 2000.
W.A. Nord	"Science, Religion, and Education." *Phi Delta Kappan*, September 1999.
Charely Reese	"Why Darwin's Theory Is in Tatters," *Conservative Chronicle*, October 20, 1999.
Michael Rustin	"A New Social Evolutionalism?" *New Left Review*, March/April 1999.

Katherine Stewart   "A Fledgling Swallow Survives the Big Bang," *Quest*, June
                      1997.

John M. Swomley   "On Creationism and Evolution," *Human Quest*,
                      March/April 2000.

Frederick Turner   "The Phony War Between Science & Religion over
                     Evolution," *American Enterprise*, September/October
                     1998.

Tom Woodward   "Meeting Darwin's Wager: How Biochemist Michael
                     Behe Uses a Mousetrap to Challenge Evolutionary
                     Theory," *Christianity Today*, April 28, 1996.

Index